"For women who are struggling with issues of body-image and self-esteem, this book is a wonderful, lovely, bedside companion for any healing journey. Its thoughtfulness is like a very thick, dark, chocolate: even one bite is powerfully satisfying. It speaks deeply to the soul. I recommend reading a chapter each night."

Beth Weinstock, PhD
Philadelphia, PA

"I had no intention of buying this book, but I'm half-way through your book and already I've gotten my money's worth. You have an understanding—not just food but all issues. I will continue to read and work through the exercises. I connect with what you have to share. Thank you for writing this!"

G.S., Minneapolis, MN

"We had to order a second copy of this book! It helps so many people who have issue with overeating and eating to cope with stress!"

Nutrition Department
Salem Hospital, OR

"I read your book and liked it a lot. One section made me cry—and I didn't know I was until tears fell on the pages! People like you are a positive force in our world."

L. J.
Devon, PA

"It is important that this material get out to women. It has been critical for my own life."

Peggy O'Mara
Mothering Magazine, Santa Fe, NM

"This is so real. How can you know so intimately what is going on inside us?!"

K.S., Student
University of Minnesota

"This is pretty powerful stuff! It really triggered me! After I read the chapters about going home, I found new and more positive ways to relate to my mother."

P.M., Wayzata, MN

"It's very important that people get the message of this book. It is fabulous—there are so many things I like about it."

Suzanne Kraemer
The Phoenix, Minneapolis, MN

"The book is so inviting—it will be a treasure for all who read it."

Ellia Manners, EEd
Cambridge, MA

"You take us right into the issues ."

C.E., Kauai, HI

"Your words spoke to my heart."

B.S., Plymouth, MN

"I like your book very much. I am using it with my students and clients."

Director of Counseling,
University of North Carolina

"My copy of your book is so used that I need another. I hope to meet you someday."

Director of Counseling,
Westpoint

Enlightened Eating™

About the Cover:

The lotus is a symbol of personal transformation and growth. Out of the deepest mud, an exquisitely beautiful flower blooms. So, too, do we grow wiser and more whole from our life experiences.

THIRD EDITION

Enlightened Eating™

Understanding and Changing Your Relationship With Food

Rebecca Ruggles Radcliffe

A Message of Wholeness & Inner Peace

EASE ™ Publications & Resources, PO Box 8032, Minneapolis, Minnesota, 55408-0032 USA

www.livingtogrow.com   *1-800-470-GROW (4769)*

Enlightened Eating™ *Understanding and Changing Your Relationship With Food*

Address All Inquiries to Publisher:
EASE™
P.O. Box 8032
Minneapolis, Minnesota, 55408-0032 USA
1-800-470-GROW (4769)
www.livingtogrow.com

ISBN 0-9636607-0-5

First Edition 1993, Second Edition 1994, Third Edition Printings: 1996, 1997, 1998, 2001
Manufactured in the United Sates of America
Designed by Beth Ruggles Design

Enlightened Eating is available to organizations for resale, patient/client resources, student textbooks, or employee/corporate gifts. Call 1-800-470-GROW (4769) to discuss quantity purchases.

Library of Congress Cataloguing-in-Publication Data

Radcliffe, Rebecca Ruggles
    Enlightened eating : understanding and changing your relationship with food /by Rebecca Ruggles Radcliffe ; design by Beth Ruggles.
       p. cm.
       ISBN 0-9636607-0-5

       1. Reducing–Psychological aspects. 2. Food habits–Psychological aspects. 3. Overweight women–Mental health.   I. Title.

RM222.2.R317 1993   613.2'5'082
                                       QBI94-2374
Library of Congress Catalog Card Number: 93-206808

Alternative Cataloguing-In-Publication Data

Radcliffe, Rebecca Ruggles
    Enlightened eating : understanding and changing your relationship with food. Design by Beth Ruggles.
3rd ed. Minneapolis, MN: EASE, copyright 2001.
    PARTIAL CONTENTS: Women in this world. Bellies, boobs, & buttocks: a closer look at body hatred. Being a survivor of sexual abuse. -Our inner spirits. -Food and feelings. -StressBreakers. A new focus: life, not food. -Surviving the holidays.

    1. Women–Eating habits. 2. Eating disorders in women. 3. Women–Body image. 4. Self-esteem in women. 5. Self-help psychology for women. 6. Minnesota literature (Nonfiction). 7. Weight control for women. 8. Overeating–Psychological aspects. 9. Overeating–Self-Treatment. I. Title. II. Title: Eating enlightened. III. Title: Understanding and changing your relationship with food. IV. EASE.

616.852 or 613.25

*This work is dedicated
to all women and their often
difficult but inspiring journeys...
and most particularly to Chloe, whose
glowing essence guides my heart. I would
not be who I am but for my daughter, my
mother, her mother, my sister, and the women
friends I love. I gratefully acknowledge the
Mother of all for nurturing and sustaining
life on this great planet. May we gently,
creatively,and respectfully nurture our
own lives and those of the
people around us.*

Dear Friend:

Life is a journey. We each have enormous potential that we never develop. At the core, we are creative, loving, vibrant, and curious beings. Through painful events and life challenges, we lose a sense of our real selves and true vision for our lives. We let go of our dreams and settle for less. These life stresses often lead to unhealthy eating patterns. We need comfort to get through difficult times, and for many, food offers a temporary fulfillment. For others, trying to not eat offers a distraction.

To get beyond a life in which food plays a central emotional role, we must begin a process of personal learning and exploration. We have to discover our needs, wishes, roadblocks, outdated thinking, and inner emotions. We need to feel the joy of discovery about what is possible in our lives and commit to an on-going process of change, step-by-step. Change is hard work. Nothing ever happens overnight. But the reward of personal growth is worth every ounce of courage and tenacity we have to muster.

ENLIGHTENED EATING™ *is dedicated to helping you make the changes you have been waiting for. While information on food, diets, and weight control can be found almost anywhere, it is rare to find real insight on why we eat and how we can begin to change the patterns and behaviors that make us feel ashamed about ourselves, our bodies, and our lives.*

ENLIGHTENED EATING™ *is full of simple, practical, and insightful articles that will remind you of what you already know, touch your heart, open up new thoughts and feelings, and point you in new directions. It is meant to be read a little at a time, feeling what it means to your life. The exercises throughout will help you discover more about yourself and your relationship to food.*

May you find the strength to explore the many possibilities for your life. Enjoy!

Warmly,

Becky

Rebecca Ruggles Radcliffe

P.S. While food issues cross all age and gender barriers, this book is written from a feminine perspective. Men will find themselves translating to their perspective while reading—just as women do quite frequently.

Contents

Introduction

"*Real change in our eating and life patterns comes about because we change how we feel inside. To do this, we have to learn more about ourselves and how we function—physically, emotionally, intellectually, and spiritually.*"

Food: The Problem, The Solution

For much of our lives we have been soothed by food. Food has made us feel content, full, and satisfied in a crazy, keyed up world. Whatever happened, we knew we could count on finding and eating a candy bar, cookie, sandwich, or chips afterwards. Maybe it wasn't right, but it helped us get by.

This pattern of reaching for food to calm and replenish ourselves is familiar to many of us. The good thing is that food is a handy and relatively inexpensive way of treating ourselves "right." The trouble is that it is expensive in other ways.

Relying too much on food to settle us down and get us through tough situations takes a toll on our bodies, our lives, and most of all, our self-esteem. Most of our bodies do not need and cannot metabolize the calories that we consume under stress. We begin to gain weight. We find ourselves getting fat.

Fat is not tolerated in today's society. It seems to say to people that we are out of control. Control, especially of the body, is held supreme. Society adores thin, athletic, and perfectly shaped bodies. It shuns large, out-of-shape individuals. Our social programming has gotten so extreme that "fat" to us can now mean being five pounds overweight!

This distaste and intolerance is turned back on ourselves. We feel the judgement of other people and in turn judge ourselves. We criticize and scold ourselves for taking that extra helping and having a snack. We feel ashamed. We hate ourselves for not being able to stop. We make promises to change and then break them everyday. We eventually stop trusting and believing in our ability to change.

Many of us reach this point early in life. If we have struggled with weight as a child, we may already feel hopeless by our early teens.

If our struggle doesn't begin until our bodies start changing, poor self-esteem could lead us to try to manage this problem of eating and body weight by starving or purging. For some, this low self-image settles in later when our bodies do not seem to be able to handle food as they used to do.

One thing is for sure—whenever and however our concerns started, they led us onto a path of endless diets, promises, and heartache. It takes our time. It undermines how we feel about ourselves.

Can this pattern be broken? Can we ever feel good about ourselves again? Can we have the hope of making peace with our bodies and with food? Of course we can. And somewhere deep inside, every one of us knows it. Every diet we go on is an attempt to break the pattern. Every healthy meal we sit down to is an attempt to break the pattern. Every internal discussion we have with ourselves is an attempt to break the pattern. We have just been going at it all wrong.

Every time we diet, we are telling ourselves we are not good enough. Every time we talk to ourselves sternly and make promises to change, we make ourselves feel ashamed of who we are and what we have done. Every time we eat a healthy meal without changing the basis for our patterns, we find ourselves right back where we started.

Very few of us are motivated by criticism. When we feel criticized, we need to be comforted—even if we are criticizing ourselves.

Instead, real change in our eating and life patterns comes about because we change how we feel inside. To do this, we have to learn more about ourselves and how we function—physically, emotionally, intellectually, and spiritually. Our minds, bodies, feelings, and spirits all have very important parts to play in our growth and development as people. We do not learn much about this in schools, churches, synagogues, or on-the-job. That means we have to teach ourselves.

There are many others who can help us through the learning process. We hear their voices in books, lectures, everyday conversations, therapy sessions, and life coincidences.

If we are open to learning about ourselves, our eating, and the way we live, we will naturally find that we are attracted to new ideas or insights that will be right for us. This process keeps repeating, helping us to gently adjust our thinking, reactions, and choices.

Over time, we learn a new style of living and coping. It never happens overnight. If it did, it would be too much of a shock to adjust to. We have to ease into change. It is the only healthy way.

Perhaps the hardest thing we have to do is cultivate patience. This is also part of our

learning process. It is based on acceptance and forgiveness, mostly of ourselves, and also of other people and circumstances that may have been hurtful.

This collection of articles is dedicated to that change. It is dedicated to helping each of us learn more about who we are and making the changes that feel right. It is based on the belief that we are all highly intelligent, creative beings who are only just beginning to wake up to our own potentials.

We are going to sow the seeds one by one, growing at our own pace and in our own direction. The light at the end of the tunnel promises that we can become happier, more peaceful, and more radiant people. As we learn to love and take care of ourselves better, we will find that our goodwill naturally extends to others and to the earth that supports us. This is the vision. Now let us begin the journey, one step at a time.

Women In This World

"*However it happens, we must honor the desire to become whole. At our deepest, we want to be loving and full of light. We want our lives to be full of creativity and happiness. We want to be with people who accept and respect us. We want to be able to express our talents and ideas freely and without fear. We want the peacefulness of self-acceptance and pleasure of sharing who we are. With each change, we come to know ourselves better and know what we need.*"

Day By Day

Each of us is an expert at change—however, most of us do not recognize this amazing ability of ours.

Think about it: we have handled countless situations through our lives. From the time we were figuring out how to crawl to the time we had to learn how to get more of our needs met in relationships or at work, we have been changing and growing every minute of our lives.

This is very creative work! It takes vision, understanding, thoughtfulness, endurance, and hope. Most of all, it takes courage.

Experts At Change

Change is the nature of life. Change is what makes us become more of who we are. Personal change is the most important work we can be doing because it lets us contribute more to the people and world around us.

However, change can make our lives feel turbulent—like we are living in the midst of a personal earthquake! It is not always easy handling what comes our way. Our tendency is to hang on and try to settle things down.

Too much change can make us feel tired and even like giving up. For those of us who struggle with food and eating problems, change adds stress which often makes us overeat, binge, purge, or restrict. How do we handle the seemingly endless stream of challenges and changes in our lives?

First of all, we recognize that change is absolutely essential to our happiness. Without any change in our lives, we would never grow. We would be stuck in a rut or routine that would bore us to tears. Change is what lets us develop new interests, meet new people, practice new skills, and most of all, find out more about ourselves.

Each of us has tremendous creative potential that is barely tapped. We are smarter and more capable than we think. We have better ideas than we ever admit. Our minds are always thinking and creating new ways of looking at things.

The problem is that most of this creativity and intelligence has been boxed in. From the time our parents started shaping our behavior and teachers started making us sit in orderly rows and doing things according to their schedules, the creative sides of ourselves got buried.

Welcoming Change

Most of us forgot how wonderful it is to play and find out new things. This process of learning and discovery feels so good as children—and as adults—because we are developing our own personal potentials. New situations help us discover more about ourselves. This means we need change in our lives.

Having an attitude that welcomes change means that we do not see change as the enemy. We do not just hang our heads, slump our shoulders, and pity ourselves for the burdens we are carrying. That simply makes us feel like we are victims of some cruel world that is out to make us feel crummy all the time.

Having an attitude that welcomes change means that we do not see change as the enemy.

Welcoming change is the same as welcoming an unexpected visit from a friend. We have to change some last minute plans, make room in our routines, and set aside the other things we had planned. Yes, there is some inconvenience, but there will be some unexpected joy, too.

Other changes are similar. Even though we are going to have to adjust our plans and expectations, some unexpected learning will come out of this. If we have a positive and open mindset, it will help us get through the challenge much better.

We have to have a little faith in our capability to adapt—(remember, we have done it many times before!)—because we may not be able to see yet what good things will come of this. Sometimes it takes a good long while to really understand how this experience is essential for our growth.

A Little Faith

Even though we need change in our lives because it helps us learn, too much can be so stressful that we no longer know how to handle it and feel overwhelmed. This damages our self-esteem.

Ideally, we want to have enough change so we are challenged to grow, but not so much that we feel helpless and defeated. Needless to say, we often cannot control how much change we face.

We can control things such as when to look for a job, break up with someone, move, take a class, and so on. If too many other things are going on, delaying major undertakings like these may be wise.

The problem usually arises when the unexpected happens—when a family member gets seriously sick or injured, we lose our jobs, someone breaks up with us, a best friend moves, we have an accident, and so on. Even small, unexpected changes add stress to life. When the unexpected changes are large, it can cause real chaos.

Developing an open attitude toward change will be helpful, but it will not get us through really difficult times. We need a practical way to handle changes when they come all at once, or when we have some kind of catastrophe in our lives. We must learn to make the changes in small increments rather than all at once. What does this mean?

Take It Day By Day

When some enormous life challenge faces us—a divorce, death, or other sudden loss—it usually feels way too big to handle. We feel like we are going to be crushed. That feeling is not unreal. When something really big faces us, we actually do not know how to handle it. If we try to imagine ourselves feeling okay again and knowing what to do, it is impossible. So how can we do it?

We take it day by day. Sometimes we have to take it hour by hour or even minute by minute. What this means is we avoid thinking we have to figure it all out right now. It may take a while. It may take a long, long while. That is okay.

What we need to focus on is getting through the first day. After we do that, we focus on getting through the next day. And so on, and so on. Eventually, we will begin to get some perspective on how we are going to survive under these new circumstances. But we do not have to have that now. At first, we just need to figure out what will make us able to handle things today.

Taking a huge life challenge day by day has been practiced and proven as a successful approach by the millions of people who have gone into treatment for addictions. They know that success sometimes means just getting through the next few minutes. This practice often works just as well for those of us who are coping with eating problems and other life changes.

Learning To Walk

This technique is really based on something that we knew as little children. When we tried to walk, we did not get up and expect to walk across the room the first time. We fell down. Then we got up and tried it again. We learned to use the furniture or other people to help us get the feel of walking which was still strange and unfamiliar.

Before we tried to walk, we felt the solid floor under our hand and knees. It felt safe. Now we were trying to navigate much further away from the ground. What a challenge! We did it step by step, day by day.

When we finally learned to walk, we could only go a few steps before falling down. But we were proud! This was fun! Once we could stay upright, then we had to learn to run and climb steps. The process was a long one, but truly worth the effort.

Handling any huge change is the same. It is like learning to walk again. And our learning is only going to happen in small baby steps—we will make mistakes and then try again.

A Vote Of Confidence

Sometimes we let our pride get in the way. We think that adults should know everything. We are really hard on ourselves for not being able to handle this. We might even think we have the right to complain because this is too big for anyone to handle.

These reactions do not get us anywhere and only prevent our creative sides from finding new solutions. Instead, we feel ashamed that we don't know the answers already. This self-condemnation often causes us to eat.

If we can shrug our shoulders and then get on with learning to handle this challenge in the most positive way possible, we give ourselves the gift of life. We are saying to ourselves that we believe we can ultimately handle this. We may not know how, but we are going to get through this. That vote of self-confidence goes a long way toward helping us heal and grow.

Exercise: *Take out your journal and make a special list of all of the changes you have gone through in your life. Start with the big ones. Alongside each change, list the positive outcomes that happened from the experience. Even if the experience was unpleasant, chances are that you got stronger or learned to understand something or someone better. Give yourself credit for all the personal learning you have already accomplished!*

If you like, continue with the smaller changes. You may begin to find a pattern to your growth as if you are on a journey in which every event leads to more self-discovery.

Bellies, Boobs, & Buttocks: A Closer Look At Body Hatred

It's that time again. Shorts, swimming suits, tank tops, and mini's.

Every magazine features tips on slapping our bodies into perfect shape in 10 easy workouts. Diet ads are everywhere, promising to get rid of our cravings or help us lose the weight if we simply give them a week.

Some of us have been getting ready for months. We dreaded the idea of exposing our bodies to the scrutiny of friends, family, or even strangers—unless they were perfect. So we started diets and exercise regimens designed to finally help us get into size six bikinis.

All we wanted was to be able to walk out with pride. We were tired of the shame we felt looking in the mirror. (Actually, disgust was more like it.) Why, why, why won't our bellies ever lie flat or our thighs appear smooth? For years we have been trying to get it right. It has just never worked.

In our society today, attractiveness means thinness. So to please others and get attention, many of us begin to focus on body weight and size.

More Than Our Bodies

Time out. What are we really saying? Why is it that women are spending all of this time dieting and trying to reshape their bodies? Why is it that even young girls are worried if they are too fat? Why is it that we cannot accept ourselves? Why is it that our bodies are so linked to our self-esteem?

Clearly, we all believe we are more than our bodies. We know we are smart, have various talents, and are good friends. We have dreams and hopes for being very successful, happy, and loved.

We know our personalities are completely unique. We are completely different than any other human being. Shouldn't that be fascinating and wonderful? Shouldn't that be what people see? So why do we get so stuck on our bodies?

We get stuck on body size and shape because of the messages we get all around us. From the time we are very little, we are reinforced for being pretty and cute. As we grow and become young women, we find ourselves the object of attention from the opposite sex. In our society today, attractiveness means thinness. So to please others and get attention, many of us begin to focus on body weight and size.

Most of the images we see around us are unrealistic. Even when we first played with Barbie dolls, we were getting unrealistic images of what grown up women are supposed to look like. Those unbalanced impressions continued when we picked up fashion and women's magazines.

A Quiet Pain

The bodies we see in magazines, catalogues, advertisements, television, and movie screens are unattainable for most of us. Most of these women are models. The average size and shape of models represents bodies that only five percent of the female population has. That means that 95 percent of us think we are fat and imperfect!

There is something very wrong in this equation. If 95 percent of people thought they were stupid, we would be worried that we were doing something damaging in schools. Yet very few people are aware of how widespread this body hatred is.

Why? Because for most of us, it stays relatively quiet. We feel it when we stand in front of a mirror or try on clothes. We feel uncomfortable walking into a room. We try to manage our feelings by beginning diets to lose five pounds or more. This pattern may go on for years, diet after diet.

For some females, their discomfort is too much to live with. They have been teased by their fathers, brothers, or boyfriends just one too many times. They feel left out or unnoticed. They have sometimes even been abused.

Whatever the triggering factors, some women begin a much more vigorous program of dieting and exercise which often leads to an eating disorder. This may begin an anorexic regimen of food restriction or a bulimic cycle of binging to fulfill hunger and purging calories that add fat. It may lead to a pattern of compulsive eating or overeating to deal with feelings of shame and inadequacy.

Set Up To Fail

Whatever the pattern, most females in this society share an underlying feeling of dislike about their bodies. This translates into a lack of self-esteem—and even a dislike of themselves as people.

Unfortunately, there is little chance of things changing around us very soon. Some say models today have more curves—but they spend five hours a day in the gym to get them.

If we become conscious of how unrealistic the images around us are, we can recognize how torturous we are to ourselves as we try to get and stay thin.

We are asking ourselves to attain what may be impossible for our body frames and metabolisms. We are setting ourselves up for failure. We are sure to feel that we will never measure up. Therefore, it is easy to think we do not deserve the love and attention we desire.

What we need instead is hope and self-acceptance. For once, females are getting a real chance to try new roles and activities. We are finding out how smart and capable we really are. We are trying different careers, starting businesses, and taking on major responsibilities outside of the home. We should be feeling fantastic about ourselves! Instead, we are feeling overwhelmed. It is understandable. There are so many new roles and expectations. Maybe this is why we turn to our bodies.

Seeking Control

Maybe it seems simpler to focus on trying to lose five pounds than getting a better job or working on an unhealthy relationship. Maybe we can feel some real success when we do lose weight—and it might be easier to get recognition for it from others than for doing something well at work or home.

The question is, are we going to let ourselves get stuck there? Even if our lives seem full of unfair and unmanageable things, are we going to settle for personal satisfaction being defined by our bodies?

Then we don't give ourselves credit for who we are. And that is the key. Society may reward us faster for being thin than for being capable, interesting, and creative. However, we don't have to accept that as the only way to think about things.

We can begin to notice other things about ourselves that we can like. We can tell ourselves we like things about our personalities, values, abilities, and behaviors. This may sound silly, but we need to hear positive feedback about ourselves.

If our friends, families, coworkers, and bosses are not telling us how special we are, then we have to tell ourselves. They may just not be capable of giving compliments. They may feel negatively about themselves, too. Many people do.

Complimenting Ourselves

Ultimately, feeling good about ourselves comes from inside. By telling ourselves we like something we did or who we are, we are helping to build self-appreciation. This increases our self-acceptance and self-esteem. Doing it once is not enough. Telling ourselves that we like who and what we are is something we need to do again and again. This positive reinforcement of ourselves eventually becomes a natural part of the way we live because we truly do like and appreciate ourselves.

At first, we just have to dare to try telling ourselves one, small, positive thing. It may be helpful to do this with a close and trusted friend. You can support each other while you are learning to reinforce yourselves.

You can do this for your body, too. You can notice parts of your body that you think are nice and compliment yourself. You may only be able to start with your hair or hands, but it is a beginning.

It may be helpful to observe bodies of other people as non-judgementally as possible. Notice a curve or use of color you like. As you look, you will see an endless stream of shapes and sizes of bodies. It is hard to believe or accept that one tall, slim, magazine shape is the only thing that can be considered beautiful.

Exercise: *Take an inventory of your body. Make a list of the parts you like and the parts you do not like. Identify why you like the parts that you do. Then identify why you do not like some other parts.*

You may find some powerful emotions associated with various parts of your body. You may have had some painful or humiliating experiences that you have tried to forget.

Close your eyes and visualize that part in your mind. Tell that part that you forgive it for not being perfect. Tell it that you will be more accepting of it from now on. See it bathed in light. Send it your love and acceptance.

Emotional Change: Approaching The Abyss

Most of us go through our early lives unaware of how we have adapted to the experiences that we have had. It often takes a traumatic event of some sort to wake us up to the fact that we may, even as adults, be reacting to painful events that we had as children or adolescents. This revealing insight often marks the beginning of a personal search for who we really are and why.

Many of us have no inkling about how our personalities have been shaped by the people and events around us, particularly in our very earliest years. We go through our infancy and early childhood dependent on our caretakers, full of innocence and trust.

Trust Is Violated

Sometimes that trust is violated directly or indirectly, intentionally or unintentionally. Parents split up. A family member dies. Someone gets very ill. There are financial troubles. This causes tension in the family and affects the quality of caretaking for children.

Worse yet, if a parent is not equipped emotionally to nurture or is struggling with an addiction or mental illness, children may feel true neglect. They may even be physically or sexually abused by family members who may be repeating what happened to them.

When something painful happens to a little child, the child reacts from what she can understand at that point. The pain is real. And it often feels overwhelming or maybe even life threatening.

Being so young and inexperienced, a little baby or child has no way to understand the pain, what her parents are feeling, or why bad things are happening. She just knows it hurts. She wants it to stop. She wants to feel safe and loved.

Memories Hold The Pain

The feeling, so big and so awful, goes into her memory. It doesn't just vanish. What also goes into her memory is her understanding or interpretation of what happened. The event is remembered from her perspective at that age.

Since a parent leaving or not caring can actually feel dangerous to a very little person who is dependent on receiving care from others, she feels completely threatened. Her helplessness and dependence is enormous. She is so frightened. She doesn't know what to do.

She may react in various ways. She may pull away, try to protect herself, feel betrayed or abandoned, take on guilt, and make inner promises or decisions to behave differently hoping to avoid a repeat experience.

Her memory also stores these reactions. It stores how she decided to do what she did. Her thinking may be simplistic, but it is the only thing she can figure out: *Mommy doesn't love me. I'll try to be good. Then she'll love me.*

As we accumulate more stress and pain in our lives, it gets harder to cover everything up. That is why eating problems, alcohol and drug abuse, violence, workaholism, and gambling are so common.

A new day comes and she hopes it will be different. She goes back to crawling, playing, and learning. She hopes the terror and pain are gone for good. She wants to forget about it. Eventually, she does. New days and new events, both good and bad, cover over the memory. But they never erase it. This cycle of pain, reaction, and stored memory repeats itself again and again as we grow up.

The Missing Element

What is missing from this cycle is a fourth step—that of healing and release. The memories remain and hold a "charge" which can affect our lives until that charge is understood (healed) and released.

A charge is an emotional energy that is stored. The emotional energy has the very same qualities as the feelings in the original experience. These feelings were stressful. They still are stressful.

The nature of the body and mind is to release stress. When the body is infested with a virus, it creates a reaction to get rid of it. When the unhealthy intruder is a painful memory, the body and mind also create reactions to get rid of it. The mind keeps going over and over an experience. The body will eventually get sick if the conscious mind doesn't have the opportunity to work through the problems.

That is why we often have the feeling as if something is bugging us, but we can't say what it is. Something indeed is bothering us, but we have learned to cover up painful memories rather than deal with them.

When we were children, that was the only thing we could do. Now that we are older, we are smart enough to see things from broader perspectives. We actually can think and feel things through to release the pain. But most of us do not know how. So we keep reacting in the same old way—we get hurt and we cover up the pain.

As we accumulate more stress and pain in our lives, it gets harder to cover everything up. That is why eating problems, alcohol and drug abuse, violence, workaholism, and gambling are so common.

Control Breaks Down

There is no place in our western society in which we learn about emotions, what they are, what they mean, and how to handle them. We learn to develop our minds and control our feelings. Since feelings really can't be controlled, we try to stuff, quiet, or block out emotions instead.

At some point, our ability to control breaks down. Our feelings leak out and our world falls apart. This usually happens at a time of crisis. A divorce, move, split, illness, rejection—anything that feels like a major trauma—can open the crack. Suddenly, a person feels as if she is out of control. Her perfectly managed life is no longer manageable.

At these key junction points, she faces two choices. This person can renew her efforts to control her feelings, numb her pain, and manage her life without confronting her problems. This inevitably will lead to more addictive behaviors of one sort or another.

Her other choice is to turn toward her pain. This choice takes a great deal of courage. She is going to try to find out what is disturbing her.

Eventually, she makes this choice because she knows that there is really no other way. By running and hiding from her feelings, she is living an unhealthy and emotionally dead life. She can't feel anything. She is never happy. She can't have any hope for things getting better because she won't let herself grow.

If she turns and faces her fears, at least she knows she is changing something. With change comes the possibility for living a new life.

The frightening part is that she is going to face the very memories that she has blocked out. She is going to remember the hurt she felt in the past. She may remember the utter emptiness of neglect. She may remember the horrible details of abuse inflicted on her or others close to her.

Remembering The Hurt

None of this is easy. It is by far the most courageous act she has probably ever done. But it is also an act of power. She is finally taking control of her life in a very real way.

She is doing something to release the intense grip of her past on her present day life. Her biggest fear when turning to face these inner demons is that once she takes the lid off, she will lose all control and go crazy. But she is stronger now. She is older and more experienced. She has already lived through the experiences once and survived. She will certainly live through them again, but this time, she can heal.

The focus on healing is critical. There is no sense in opening old pain just to sink into it. No one wants to feel pain. The point in going back and looking at painful memories is that as adults, we have the capacity now to understand what happened.

We can give credit where credit is due. We have the capacity to forgive the little children inside us who did the best they could to handle the terrible things they were feeling. We can even gain a realistic perspective about the people who caused the pain.

Healing The Past

Much of this emotional work is best done with someone who is skilled at helping us learn to sort through past experiences and understand them in a new light. These counselors and therapists help us feel safe enough to feel what we were so afraid of feeling. With their help, we can release the pain and go on with our lives.

Once we have begun emotional healing of past wounds and their effects on the present, we begin to recognize how much of our lives are colored by early experiences. We learn to notice when something is bothering us. We know how to examine what the feelings are and learn how to deal with them constructively.

Preparing to do memory work may feel like we are approaching an abyss. By working with a skilled therapist, we are guided back gently and carefully to pieces of the memories. Rarely do we get everything all at once. It would be too much of an overload. By working with impressions and the details that are remembered, over time, more comes out.

Eventually, enough is remembered so that the person can rework how she feels about what happened. She is finally free of the burden of that memory. She can release her self-blame and go on with her life. This is true healing.

Exercise: *Take your journal and write down some key memories of childhood. What is your earliest memory? Identify memories related to areas that are problems in your life.*

For example, if you struggle with food, write down all of the memories you have from your childhood relating to food. Keep a special place in your journal for this memory list. Over time, you may remember new things, especially as you return home or attend holiday or family meals. Talk with other family members to see what they remember.

You may uncover some very important clues that have contributed to your personal abuse of food. Remember, you may find painful memories. Work closely with your counselor or therapist. If you don't have one, this may be time to start.

Starting Tomorrow, Things Will Be Different

One of the most frustrating things about having a problem relationship with food is that we can't ever seem to keep a promise. Every day we wake up hoping today will be the day we change. Every Monday we hope we are inspired enough to start anew. Every birthday, every new season, every new year, and most of all, after every binge.

The endless disappointment we feel is hard to live with. We have no one else to rely on but ourselves in this battle of willpower over food. If we keep losing the battle, how can we ever truly hope to change?

Endless Disappointment

This disappointment turns back inward upon ourselves. We begin to believe that we are not trustworthy—that we really cannot rely on ourselves. These thoughts grow stronger with every binge and every broken promise.

They turn into self-doubt first, and then into a lack of self-confidence. Every time we make a promise to ourselves, another voice inside sarcastically says, *Sure you'll*

> *We begin to believe that we are not trustworthy—that we really cannot rely on ourselves. These thoughts grow stronger with every binge and every broken promise.*

change—just like every other time. This second nagging voice can wear us down. It takes away our hope that things will ever be better. Our self-esteem plummets even lower.

Are we wrong to make promises in the first place? Should we just give up trying? Should we accept that we are incapable of change?

Should we acknowledge that we are weak and unworthy of a better life? We begin to feel like giving up. After all, how long can someone expect to struggle against the odds without feeling any improvement?

Each one of us has to face these questions when we try to change our relationship to food. We come to a point where we feel like scum, like we deserve all of the unhappiness we feel because we cannot get out of the disgusting, depressing hole we have fallen into.

Hitting Bottom

When we hit bottom like this, it actually is a relief. We have been scared to get this low, to feel this hopeless, to get to the very edge of what we can take. Now, we can't get any lower. So what next?

This is probably where some of us wonder if the struggle is worth it—whether living is even worth the effort because there is so much pain. Thoughts of suicide or ending it all are not uncommon among individuals who have disordered, addictive relationships to food. It is easy to understand why.

So the next time you are on the bottom, take a good look around you. What are your options? What do you really feel about life? This is the time to dig into the deepest part of your soul and find out what you believe about living. Should it really be this way?

At a time like this, our pain is so strong because we know that this is not how life was meant to be. We know that there are different ways of living. We know we are capable of happiness and hope. We want to do good for ourselves and others. We have aspirations and dreams about our lives, but they can't come true if we keep on doing things this way.

The part of us that knows there is something better is the part that keeps making promises to change. It can be a very powerful partner to each of us every single day because it keeps hope alive. It keeps dreaming even when it seems silly to dream.

Stubborn Wisdom

When you are sitting on the bottom, find that side of you that is too stubborn to quit. This is your true power. Your stubbornness and refusal to give up, even when it seems crazy to think you have a chance, is what will help you begin to climb out of the hole.

The side of you that is willing to keep trying again is really your wisest side. It is the side that knows you have the potential to create a different kind of life. It may not know exactly how yet, but it refuses to quit. That angry, stubborn, defiant energy will give you the will to try again.

When we stumble and break our promises to ourselves, it is important to know that we were not foolish to make promises in the first place. Making a promise is an act of hope. Hope is the energy that takes everyone into their future. Hope is a blessing—it is necessary to live.

What we may want to look at more closely is the kind of promises we are making. Maybe we are setting ourselves up for failing because we want to change completely overnight. Our

promises may have been too big for us to accomplish in the time we allowed.

We have to be kind and realistic to ourselves as we try to change. If we let the sarcastic, disappointed, nagging voices inside bully us into thinking we have to be completely different or else we will have failed again, then we will never stand a chance.

All change takes time. Growth happens in small steps. Our first promises should be tiny, and very achievable. This way, we can feel a little pride when we keep them. Then we can muster the courage to try other small promises. Moving forward in slow, small steps rebuilds the self-trust that was beaten down so many times before.

Exercise: *Make some private time for yourself and then write a letter. The letter should be written by the side of you that thinks things should be different. Let it have a voice. Let it tell you what it believes and why it keeps trying. Be careful to not edit this voice— do not stop it if it sounds unrealistic or impossible. This is your inspired side. Inspiration is not rational or scientific. It is the passion for living. Keep this letter and read it whenever you need to be reminded of this hope. Add to the letter whenever you want.*

Out Of Darkness

Time alone is intimidating if a person hasn't chosen to be alone. The empty hours stretch on ahead. Every minute drags by reminding us of how alone we are. Time feels like a prison. We are eager to find ways to make it pass. One way is to eat.

For many people who struggle with food, time is an enemy. Time is something to combat, to conquer. We seek for ways to fill or pass it. When there is nothing around to distract us, the emptiness we are left with is very frightening.

We do not notice it when we have plenty to do. So we work very hard to keep busy—we watch TV; we hang out with people we know even if we are bored; we go shopping; we get high; we read; we work longer hours—anything to keep away the panic we feel when we are alone. We even eat.

A Secret Mess

Why is feeling alone so frightening? We are afraid that we deserve to be alone. Although our lives may look together on the outside, many of us feel worthless inside.

> *For many people who struggle with food, time is an enemy. Time is something to combat, to conquer. We seek for ways to fill or pass it.*

This is a secret that no one else would ever guess. We may be very good students, employees, friends, and companions—the kind of people everyone loves—while inside we know things are not as they should be. Something feels very wrong.

If we have been successful by everyone else's measure, why don't we feel satisfied? Getting good grades, having friends, and being liked

by our superiors isn't enough if we are only doing these things to please others.

As youngsters, particularly as little girls, we are taught to be sweet, kind, helpful, and cute. We learn that people like us when we don't make trouble and when we make them happy.

We very quickly learn to keep tabs on the people around us and adapt to please them. When they feel happy, we feel that we have done our jobs. This is called caretaking.

Many women grow up learning that caretaking is the only role they are supposed to do. If they have practiced it all of their lives, caretaking may be the only role they feel good at doing.

Making people happy can certainly make us happy, too. We feel pretty powerful and important if we can positively impact others' lives. But this gets old and leaves us feeling that something significant is missing.

What is missing is our Self—our own true and unique identities. While we grew, we missed lessons on figuring out who we were. We never figured out what we needed to be happy. In fact, we were taught that thinking about ourselves was selfish.

Consequently, we never became our own unique people. We never developed a sense of "me-ness": this is who we are, what we want, and where we fit in. Instead, we were people pleasers.

Without a sense of personal identity, we feel empty inside. Actually, we are empty. A very important void never got filled in. When we are alone, we feel uncomfortable because we sense that emptiness.

We don't know what to do. Eating fills up that void temporarily. Eating, however, doesn't fix the problem. The next quiet moment reminds us of that frightening emptiness and drives us to eat.

The Art Of Deception

We are terrified that others will find out how worthless we really are. If we have nothing inside, why would they ever find us interesting or likable? Why would they ever want to spend time with us? What would keep them in our lives?

We are afraid that the answer is "nothing," and that we would be left alone. It seems much better to keep other people around us by making them think we are terrific. Other people will never know how empty we are if they think we are wonderfully sensitive and compassionate companions.

We keep people around us through caretaking, but we never get our needs met and never figure out who we really are. Yet we are relieved that we are at least not alone—or are we?

The Missing Self

Maybe we are eating because we still feel alone even in the company of others. If they don't really know who we are, are they really with us? Are they here because they chose to be with us because we are unique? Or did they just choose to be with us because we make them feel good?

If we are caretakers, eventually we ask these questions. We become resentful and feel taken advantage of or used. Unfortunately, it is no one's fault but our own since we won them over originally with our niceness.

We have never learned to trust that people will appreciate our individuality. We were told

it would get in the way of being liked and accepted. We became good little girls instead and never grew up into adult women.

Does this have a familiar ring to it? Does this sound like we are living our mothers' lives all over again? Won't we be complaining any minute that our family and friends don't appreciate us enough? Won't we risk driving loved ones away because we are asking them to fill a void that only we can fill?

No one else can help us become unique human beings. That is a job we, as modern women, have to do ourselves. It is exciting and downright terrifying because we have to do it alone. But this kind of aloneness is not empty. Our private undertaking offers us the reward of becoming authentically unique people.

Exercise: *Imagine that you are invited to an award gala because you are going to finally receive the recognition you deserve from others. Close your eyes and imagine to the most minute detail how you would look: what you would wear, how would you do your hair and make-up, and how would you get there. Embellish the image lavishly. Now imagine each of the key people up on stage making a speech about why you deserve the award you are about to receive. Listen to the long list of reasons they cite. Notice how you are feeling as each person in your life gets up with praise for what you do for them. Make a list of these reasons—they are the benefits you get out of pleasing others.*

What Are We Going To Do When We Grow Up?

We live in an era of the greatest job potential that has ever existed for women of every age. Thanks to earlier generations who fought for greater rights and opportunities, we now assume that we can have almost any job we desire as long as we are qualified. Certainly, discrimination still exists for size, age, color, and sex. Nonetheless, there are a multitude of choices to make about the kind of work we want to do.

This is where we often get into trouble. Answering the question, *"what do I want to do when I grow up?,"* is not easy!

Career Intimidation

Suitable work can bring us personal happiness, growth, and satisfaction. Therefore, taking a look at what we are doing and whether it is right for us is an important thing to do periodically.

Whether we are just starting out, or whether we have been working for a while, thinking about a career can be intimidating. There are so many possibilities that we often don't know how to begin.

Women...are used to putting up with less because they think they don't deserve anything else.

Because looking for a job can be hard, some of us take the first thing that comes along or stay in jobs that make us unhappy. This is especially true if we already have self doubts.

Settling For Less

Women, and certainly many who struggle with issues of eating, poor body image, and low self-esteem, are used to putting up with less because they think they don't deserve anything else.

They feel unqualified to seek out something better and are scared of being rejected. So they stay put and envy others who reach out for more. They meekly accept their lot as if it were a punishment for some unknown inadequacy.

This is something every person has to deal with to some extent, but women are more prone to settle for less than their typical male counterparts.

Childhood Training

In western cultures, women have traditionally stayed home to manage the household and raise children, while men have gone off to work.

From the time children are little, they know this is so and their games reflect it. Girls play "house" and boys play cops and robbers, firemen, doctors, cowboys, etc. Boys are allowed to play louder, more roughly, and more competitively than girls, which better prepares them for a working world created by men.

Little girls are raised to care for their families. They practice loving and nurturing behaviors with their dolls and friends. They are expected to be helpful around the house and with brothers and sisters. They watch their mothers caring for family members, so they grow up believing that taking care of relationships is very important work.

The New Intruder

When women go to work, they bring these supportive and cooperative values with them. Unfortunately, they find themselves competing with other men and women. They are in a world where backstabbing and maneuvering is commonplace. This environment is unfamiliar to women and undermines relationships which they value so highly.

They work for men who still privately think women belong at home. Women constantly have to prove how good they really are, even if they are better than their male counterparts.

Scared Away

Women, just as men, prepare themselves with schooling, mentors, internships, workshops, and reading. They network to find opportunities and interview widely. They take jobs and work hard to gain responsibility and higher salaries, little by little.

The frustrating thing is that women, more than men, find that recognition and reward for their work is slower and less frequent in coming. They have to rely more on their own self-confidence. They fight harder for promotions and raises. They may have to change jobs to get the increases they deserve.

Is this fair? No. Does it make sense? Sure. The old order has been upset, and many men don't like it.

Faced with this unfriendly arena, many women are understandably reluctant to try to make a place for themselves within it because the cost is so great.

Femininity Fails

The kind, caring, sweet, meek, and insecure persona that young girls are encouraged to develop does not serve them well in this battleground of work opportunity.

An office is often characterized as a war or sporting event. Since few women have been trained in combat or team sports, they are missing specific skills. Also, women are not generally as aggressive as men, which may be due to physiological reasons as well as socialization.

Furthermore, if a woman gets up the courage to go after something she wants, she is often criticized for being uncaring, selfish, or 'bitchy'. Because as women, we value relationships so much, most of us cannot tolerate being viewed this way whether or not the criticism is deserved.

Back To The Nest

So we go home and eat. We cannot figure out these new rules and we don't like what we are feeling. Interviewing makes us eat. Deadlines make us eat. Writing resumes makes us eat. Asking for raises makes us eat. Meeting with bosses makes us eat. Competing with co-workers makes us eat. Everything feels foreign. We don't seem to belong.

Backing away doesn't help either, unfortunately. Many of us spend the biggest portion of our day at work. We sacrifice our esteem when we settle for work that doesn't challenge or suit us.

Luckily, there are an increasing number of resources for developing careers including books, adult ed classes, workshops, resource centers, and mentor programs to help with all aspects of work.

As we become healthier, it is only natural that we would want opportunities to work in healthy settings that give us the chance to make contributions and express our creativity.

We may have to work hard to find such a place, but making the effort does have its rewards. Challenging ourselves lets us find talents and strengths we never knew we had. Our self-esteem and pride can grow with every small success we have. When we thrive at work, it contributes to our sense of personal happiness.

Exercise: *Make a list of all the fantasies you have about the work you want. Make a list of all the qualities you want to develop. Make a list of the circumstances you would like to have happen. These wish lists help you dream and envision possibilities.*

Review them often. As you grow, keep your goals in mind. What are you working toward now? What more could you do to comfortably stretch yourself?

A Horrible Silence: Being A Survivor Of Sexual Abuse

There is a darkness like no other. It is deep and full of shame. No one else knows. Most of what happened is buried so far under that it is virtually forgotten. Yet it stays alive in a silent nightmare that contaminates every action, feeling, hope, and dream. This darkness is what every victim of sexual abuse lives with day in and day out.

Shattered Soul

The horror she once lived through shattered her soul. Whatever is left is in tiny little pieces. She works hard to keep herself together. Sometimes she can't. There are some days that just don't work. She can't get out of bed. She can't leave the house. She can't do anything. Most of all, she can't tell anyone.

She's desperate to turn off the feelings. They are going to swallow her whole. They threaten to overwhelm her. There would be nothing left. Just like before, she feels overpowered and terrified.

> *She's desperate to turn off the feelings. They are going to swallow her whole. They threaten to overwhelm her. There would be nothing left*

She has to find a way to shut down. These feelings have to be turned off, or she may completely fall apart.

Mountains Of Food

So she takes the first bite. And then another. Mouthful after mouthful, stuffing down the feelings: rage at having been violated; terror at being out of control; betrayal by those who were supposed to protect; grief for the loss of innocence; panic that it could ever happen again; and shame from feeling responsible.

It takes a long time to settle down. The feelings are so intense that they are not easily soothed. They tumble and rage inside with frightening ferocity. They have been caged up for so long that their power has grown too big to handle.

It takes mountains of food. No one else can be around. This is a private battle. No one else understands the pain. They would be horrified to see what happens in that darkness. No one else can ever see this attempt to quell the demons.

The battle is not easy, and the price is large. Bite after bite builds up to pound after pound. There are only two alternatives and both are intolerable: throw it all up or live with the weight.

Too Much Pain

The pain has to be stopped. Too much is at stake. She tried other things: drinking, drugs, spending, sex, and overwork. Food is safer, and for a while it works.

In the madness of binging, there comes a point when numbness takes over. Finally, all is quiet. Finally, she can sleep.

It is a sad sleep. Her relief is full of a new pain. She hates herself. She hates this secret life. She finds it disgusting, and loathes her inability to stop. She beats herself up for not being able to handle things better. She wakes up depressed. How in heaven's name is she ever going to get out of this hell?

One Way Out

There is only one way out. It is slow and difficult. The survivor of abuse lives with a story so horrible that it should never have happened to anybody. To survive, she has locked her memories so far inside that they are forgotten for a very long time.

Loss of memory is actually a protective measure for the person who suffered the original abuse. At that time, she was too small to fend off her perpetrator and the threats made her too afraid to tell anyone. To keep herself from going crazy, she blocked out the horror instead.

Unfortunately, the memories never really go away. The silent pain stays inside and affects every action and feeling the rest of her adult life. She is still a victim. She cannot trust. She is frightened that once again, someone will overpower her and make her do things that revolt her very being.

She keeps her true feelings to herself and may live reclusively. For a long time, she doesn't know why she eats. She doesn't know what is bothering her. She doesn't know why she can never be happy.

Shadows Of Memory

One day, something begins to trigger her memory. At first, there are only the vaguest sensations. Perhaps some smell or song bothers her. She is reminded of her old house. She gets too angry at someone.

This shadowy recall may go on for a very long time. It is a very important stage because it lets the victim know she can handle the feelings as they come up.

Then perhaps someday, she sees a movie in which someone is sexually abused. She hears someone talking about an abusive past, or she sees a talk show on this topic. It is unsettling. It feels too close to home, but she doesn't know why. She has nightmares. She begins to suspect, but at first denies the possibility.

Back In The Kitchen

All this time, she keeps eating. She wishes she could get in control, but no matter what she does, she finds herself back in the kitchen binging.

Then one day, she is someplace safe enough that a small, but clear memory surfaces. It might be a tiny piece: a memory of choking, the sensation of someone big over her, or remembering huddling scared in bed at night.

This first real memory can bring a flood of terror. She may fall apart. Her eating may accelerate. Hopefully, she finds someone to talk to: a rape crisis center, therapist, or trusted friend. She gets through somehow.

Slowly, over months or years, more pieces surface. Usually, the survivor now needs to find people who know exactly what she is going through. This counselor or support group provides support so that she doesn't shatter again.

Choosing To Feel

As the memories return, so does the pain. At times, it seems overpowering. It is terrifying because it reminds her of the abuse. But now, she knows how much her life is held hostage by this cruelty. Unless she frees herself by remembering, she will never have her own life back. So she chooses to keep remembering.

Her pain is enormous. Her rage is almost uncontainable. Most of all, her grief goes to the bottom of her soul. Yet, only by remembering can she see the first glimmer of light. She feels her power grow as she chooses to heal. She learns that she can count on herself. She begins to treat herself tenderly. She begins to nurture herself. It feels strange but good.

Slowly, ever so slowly, she puts the pieces of herself together. She is becoming whole for the first time. As she does, the grip of her food use loosens. She finds herself in her kitchen less often. And when she does, she knows it means that some new feelings have to be dealt with in her next group or therapy session.

She has hope, finally, for her future. She doesn't know exactly what it will be, but she knows she has one. She is setting herself free.

No More Victim Consciousness

When we are in the middle of overwhelming situations, it is natural to want to blame someone for the trouble we are in. It makes us feel better to think that someone or something else is responsible.

Unfortunately, this doesn't get us anywhere, except into conflict with whoever we blame. Blaming others has caused countless wars, lost friendships, broken romances, divorces, legal and political battles, and ruined businesses.

Out Of The Blue

We work very hard to keep our lives together. When difficult circumstances hit us out of the blue, everything we have worked for seems threatened. Our survival instincts lead us to find the threat and get rid of it.

> *When we feel like victims of circumstance, we find ourselves feeling powerless, helpless, or hopeless. Stripped of our power psycho-logically, we sit back and wait for someone else to bail us out or change things for the better.*

If our lives are full of complications, this approach could mean that we are fighting all of the time. This takes energy that could be spent on growing and doing positive things for ourselves. We are the real losers.

A Depressing View Of Life

When we fight, we feel increased stress and disappointment with life. In the long run, this can wear out our goodwill and optimism. We might come to believe that life holds very little joy, and that human beings are basically mean.

This is a very depressing view. It undermines our motivation to get up, take charge, and change things for the better because

someone is just going to come along and ruin them anyway.

A Fact Of Life

Living does require taking risk. There is simply no way to control every possible factor that could affect our plans. Risk is something we are all very used to. Simply leaving the house in the morning or driving down the road involves risk. Staying locked up in our homes does not prevent us from falling victim to storms, theft, illnesses, etc.

When we feel like victims of circumstance, we find ourselves feeling powerless, helpless, or hopeless. Stripped of our power psychologically, we sit back and wait for someone else to bail us out or change things for the better. We hole up, protecting our tender selves from insult, humiliation, neglect, or pain. We hope that by hiding, we will avoid further bruising.

Victims Of Circumstance

If we really are the intended targets of hurtful actions from other people, then we need to muster enough courage any way we can to change our circumstances as quickly as possible.

More often, we feel like victims because we have been victimized in the past and have learned to expect to be hurt. Every time our lives take unexpected turns, our fears rise back up, and we back down. By reacting to every situation as if we are going to get battered, we allow other people to take control, steering our lives in directions we may not want to go.

We give them the opportunity to take charge—whether they want to or not—merely because we do not assert ourselves in any way. We don't make our preferences, ideas, goals, or needs known. By burying ourselves, we miss a lot of living. Other people end up running our lives because we don't take responsibility for them ourselves.

Responsibility requires action, and we are frozen scared.

Each of us makes a choice every time we do something: Are we willing to try this even though something might interfere with our plans in some way, or aren't we?

It's All In The Attitude

The attitude we take toward unplanned change determines whether we feel like we are victims or not. We can bet our last dollars that no matter what we plan, things will end up differently than we imagined. Dates, weddings, new jobs, relationships, trips, parties, weekend plans—nothing ever turns out exactly as planned.

The question is, are we going to get upset at the change or can we learn to expect the unexpected? If we take a change in plans as a normal life occurrence, then we will not be as surprised or disappointed. We will won't need to find fault as quickly with other people.

Enjoying The Surprise

Expecting the unexpected can take two different tones. We can become cynical and always expect something to ruin our plans. We can also expect things to simply be different and enjoy the surprise when it presents itself.

Obviously, the first approach is so negative that it offers no improvement. On the other hand, learning to enjoy life's surprises requires that we have a playful attitude. Living is like watching a movie where we don't know the ending, but we enjoy finding out.

Weathering A Crisis

What about the times when real trouble rains down on us? Car accidents, the death of a parent, a serious illness, bankruptcy, an unexpected pregnancy, losing a job, failing school, having to move to a new town, etc., all take enormous amounts of energy and have long-reaching impact.

In the middle of the crisis, we are only concerned about surviving the trauma. As time passes, we have a chance to see ourselves become stronger as a result of these painful events. We look back and realize that we are able to do things we would never have dared before. In the long run, difficult challenges enable us to develop our potential. What was once negative, now is positive.

Growing Stronger

In the middle of a crisis, this realization makes it easier to believe that something positive will result over time. Some people find this so true that they believe every experience is meant to be.

Believing that you are being challenged so you can grow is a much more positive way of seeing life than feeling like you are callously tossed into trouble because someone or something screwed up.

You can use every opportunity to get stronger and wiser. You review each situation for what it can teach you. You feel in charge of your attitude and response even if you cannot control the circumstances. You are willing to face the surprises that are sure to come. You are willing to grow.

Exercise: Take out your journal and fill in as many answers to each of the following statements as possible:

If __x__ hadn't happened, I would not be able to _____

If __x__ hadn't happened, I would not have done _____

I am stronger because_____

I am who I am today because_____

Healing At Our Own Pace

We live in a rush-rush society. People seem impressed with us when we are trying to juggle 23 balls all at the same time. We talk about how many reports we have to write, the extra projects we are doing, the social life we are keeping, and our crazy schedules. We barely have time to do anything for ourselves unless it is on the run.

We are victims of a get-ahead mentality. For generations, people have been trying to better themselves. They have pursued higher education, greater wealth, increased status, and more recognition. For the past 30 years, this has meant the right schools, the right friends, the right extra-curricular activities, and the right jobs. Lately, it also means the right look, the right body, and the right clothes.

Getting Superficial

We are getting more and more superficial as the pace steps up. Life zooms along faster, and so our moment to make the right impression is smaller. To compete, we feel

Changing our lives—whether the change is big or small—means slowing down to think and feel.

that we have to buy into the game. So we get good grades, do the right internships, and get the proper recommendations and introductions to get us into commendable jobs. We are off and running, and we never stop.

We have learned that to get ahead we have to keep going and to impress. We have to ski, volunteer, play tennis, look fabulous in a bikini, and know how to cook (but never put on weight)—all without seeming

stressed or unhappy. Successful people always seem happy. So we keep ourselves cheerful to get ahead, be accepted, and feel good about ourselves.

What a tiring way to live! It certainly seems exciting—and if one's energy can truly keep up with a multitude of demands, then a whirlwind style of living may be fun. But for those who have underlying stresses, conflict, and old wounds, a lifestyle like this takes its toll.

Something Back

When we put out a lot of energy, it has to be replenished in some way. Just as the well runs dry unless more water comes from somewhere, it is the same with us. We give and give to our work, friends, homes, families—and even our bodies.

Does it come back to us? Is our work rewarding? Do we feel satisfied and happy at the end of the day, or are we just tired? Do we feel rejuvenated after being with our friends because their loving attention nourishes us, or are we doing all the giving? Do we feel cozy and peaceful where we live, or is it just a place to put our things? Do we feel safe and connected with our family, or are we alone even when we are with them?

If the energy we put out comes back in a circle and fills us up with good feelings, then we are clearly on a healthy track. We have learned to choose activities that nourish our minds, hearts, and bodies. This is indeed a lucky way to live.

Living Off Track

Too many of us feel tired and out of sorts much of the time. Our days do not have purpose and our activities are not personally rewarding. We are on a crazy treadmill that never stops. There isn't time to think. We just keep blindly pushing ahead. We try to do the right things and never question why they don't feel right.

Changing our lives—whether the change is big or small—means slowing down to think and feel. We have to become aware of who we are at that moment: what are our real needs...what is really going on...what the real problem is...what change needs to happen...and how we can take the first step.

Getting Clear

To figure all of this out, our minds have to be quiet enough to think. Our hearts have to be quiet enough to feel. Our souls have to be quiet enough to speak. Only then can we really know what we should do.

We cannot be that quiet unless we slow down. Racing around like maniac achievement addicts will get us more notice and less peace. If we want to be truly healthy, whole people, it won't happen at 500 miles per hour when all we can do is simply hang on for dear life.

Paying Attention

If life is really dear to us, we need to treat it with care and compassion. If a little child you care about is hurting, you stop what you are doing, give her your full attention, and in a very gentle way, find out what is wrong.

Just because we are grown up little girls doesn't mean we don't need to have someone bend down and take time to find out what is making us hurt. We need that same loving attention.

Since it is hard to count on anyone else doing it for us because we are supposed to

be responsible people, we have to do this gentle intervention for ourselves.

Concern Must Be Genuine

We need to stop what we are doing, at least occasionally, and talk to the person that lives inside of our busyness. If our concern for ourselves is legitimate, then this inner part of us will feel safe coming forward to let us know what is going on.

If we would rather get on with everything else we have to do, then we may feel irritated that we have to bother with our feelings and wishes. We will stop only for a second, and we won't hear anything. Our inner being senses that the concern is not genuine. There is no real commitment to change.

Time To Heal

Once we know what needs to change in our lives—for example, if we want to create a different relationship to food—we have to step out of the rat-race and make time and space to heal.

This may mean letting go of things that we thought were important. It may mean working less hours or taking fewer classes. It may mean not hanging out with friends as often or exercising as much. We need to make time to hear ourselves and reshape our lives.

Changing our lives takes an enormous amount of emotional and physiological energy. It is the most difficult work we will ever do. Yet most of us try and do it on the side: we squeeze it in, slip in a therapy session in between other appointments, and think about what is going on just before going to sleep.

We can change this way, but it will be in tiny, tiny, slow increments. We are likely to get discouraged because nothing will seem to be happening.

Commitment Counts

If we want to see results, we have to be as committed to personal change as we are to anything else we undertake. We think nothing of dedicating several hours a week to shaping our bodies with exercise, counting calories, or putting on clothing and make-up to create the right effect.

We make time for important things. Our personal change just has to become equally important to us. Then we can build in time to listen to ourselves every day, practice new choices, learn as we go, and notice and celebrate the progress we make.

Exercise: *Try building in some daily quiet time to hear what is really going on in your life. You must find a private place and make sure that you will be uninterrupted. (Find a stall in a library. Sit in your car. Pour a bath and lock the door. Go for a walk in a park, etc.) Take at least 20 minutes. If you feel out of sorts, begin to describe what might be going on. If you know what you'd like to change, explore what holds you back and how you can begin to overcome those obstacles. Change never happens overnight. As you think or write, be gentle and ask what small thing you could begin with today. What one, small, doable change would feel good today. As much as possible, honor that request. The next day, think or write about what happened when you tried to do the one small change. If you learned that you need to do something else first, then identify that small change for the next day. Repeat the process day by day. Always be kind. Inside, we are still those same little girls. We will scare easily and quit unless we are very, very gentle.*

Getting Ready To Say Goodbye

Each of us faces moments when we finally know that something is over. It is often a sad moment, full of letting go. Even though we know that we have to move on, we often linger, checking out our decision, hoping that something will change last minute, and trying to find out if we were wrong to decide to leave. Yet the truth keeps staring us in the face, waiting for us to take the next step in our lives.

What will it be? Where will we go? What will we do? How will we feel? No wonder we are reluctant to get up and get moving. The changes ahead seem overwhelming and completely without answers. We retreat for a while, back into our familiar routines. We are safe here in the present. We know the rules. We know what to expect. We know the pitfalls.

Without A Clue

Out there in the new tomorrow, we don't have a clue about anything! Who will be our allies? Who will be there for us when we need to turn to someone? What will inspire us? What will keep us going? We take our first steps out of complete faith that somehow, some way we will find new paths to follow.

Leaving Our Loves

Occasionally, the changes we require of ourselves—or that our growth requires of us—are small. We find ourselves changing routines, tossing out old things in the attic, or taking up hobbies such as music. Sometimes the changes are much more dramatic. We find ourselves choosing to leave our boyfriends...our parents' homes or value systems...jobs that are no longer healthy for us...roommates that can't support our needs...or behaviors that we have outgrown.

These people, places, or activities have been a part of our lives. We have given them significant time, attention, life energy, and commitment. Now that we find ourselves needing to leave, we feel full of grief—even though we know we are completely ready and willing to move on.

This is the process of saying goodbye. We unwind our minds, hearts, bodies, and souls from the entanglements we have with this phase of our lives. It is over. We are sad. We wish it was otherwise, but it is not. So we keep unwinding. And the tears come to help us cleanse the remaining tension we might feel. We release the old and move on to the new.

Our Helpers Change

We cannot take everyone and everything on the next stage of our personal journeys. We have specific needs that are fostered and nurtured by certain personalities, values, and experiences. As we change, so do our helpers along the way. A different job brings out new abilities or a new level of confidence. A new roommate opens the door to new interests and people. Different apartments let us create our space all over

> *Now that we find ourselves needing to leave, we feel full of grief—even though we know we are completely ready and willing to move on.*

again to fit the changes we are making in our personal lives. Different partners support the healthy decisions we make rather that perpetuate the old ones.

As we make room for new resources, the old ones fall away. Some of them were completely unhealthy, so we are glad to see them go. Others we wish we could keep. Of course, it is easier not to have to change: it takes so much energy to adjust to a new job or situation.

Sometimes, there are people we must part from that we dearly want to hang onto—such as a special friend or lover that meant a great deal to us. Yet now, they don't seem to understand these new choices we are making. They drift away, and we find it hard to connect anymore.

No Way To Stop

The truth is, we can't stop changing even if we wanted to. We can't go back to our old ways or pretend that we are the same old person. It might work for a short time, but the pretense always breaks down. Eventually, everyone sees through the act. Worst of all, we don't feel true to ourselves while we try to stay the same.

It simply isn't worth the internal pain of denying our changes. After all, it is our inner selves that remain the most faithful throughout every single change of our lives. Anything and everything else can change. Everyone else can move on, too. But our internal being stays steadfast. Each of us is the same inner person we have been since we were a child. We are just older, more aware, and hopefully, a bit stronger. If we deny our connection to the change that stems from this inner process, then we are deserting ourselves in a very deep way.

So, when we face significant turning points, we must let ourselves move on. We will find ourselves under a new sky. The horizon will be different. The landscape will be unknown. But there are others who can be our companions for this new phase.

So far, no one knows of any shortcut to this process. There is simply no easy way to say goodbye. Each time we face the unknown, we quake at the knees. We are sure we won't survive. How can we be? We cannot see anything that is coming. We move forward with blind faith, and it is terrifying.

Empty Without Change

Yet it has to be done. Without moving on, we stagnate. Our growth comes to a halt and we fester. We become irritable and hopeless. Eventually, we turn nasty or become invisible— we know this isn't right, but we have forgotten that change requires personal courage. When we stop changing, our souls no longer vibrate or feel alive.

It is possible to resist change. We can do it by denying our natural urges to grow. We can refuse to act on our curiosity. We can stop taking new routes. As we find ourselves dissatisfied, we can cover our feelings over in some way. We can eat. Drink. Party. Work. Space out in front of the television. But as time passes, it will take more food, alcohol, and television to cover over the doubts we have about not changing.

Getting By Or Being Alive

It is really a question of how we are going to live. Are we going to find out who we really are? Or are we going to just get by however we can? If we want to feel truly alive, then we are going to have to move on whenever we outgrow something.

We will know when this happens. It is not an arbitrary thing. We hear voices of dissatisfaction inside. Or we hear voices of curiosity leading us forward. We have thoughts that won't let us alone. Or we make new discoveries in therapy.

Becoming Whole

However it happens, we must honor the desire to become whole. At our deepest, we want to be loving and full of light. We want our lives to be full of creativity and happiness. We want to be with people who accept and respect us. We want to be able to express our talents and ideas freely and without fear. We want the peacefulness of self-acceptance and pleasure of sharing who we are. With each change, we come to know ourselves better and know what we need.

To the best of our abilities, we must honor those needs. Oftentimes, we can proceed onward with our lives without making monumental changes. But every once in a while, we will be called upon by our souls to make an enormous shift in our lives—to make room for a whole new wave of personal development.

When we find ourselves in the midst of one of those goodbyes, we can comfort ourselves with the knowledge that something significant is in the wind for us. We will look back from the days ahead to this time and know that we are no longer who we once were—and that we never could have become the people we are today without going through these major changes.

Exercise: *At many points in our growth, we find ourselves saying goodbye to something. When you find yourself sad or reluctant to let go of a person, place, or behavior, sit down and write a love letter to it/him/her. Really pour out your feelings without censoring them. No one else need read this. You do not have to send it. But you may be surprised to find how important this "friend" was to you and understand better why it is so hard to leave.*

Following The Feminine

*W*omen have a very hard role to play in the world because their differences and values are not recognized. Women have the great gift of being attuned to the needs and feelings of others—and of healing those feelings: women recognize when someone is feeling bad, and they do everything they can to make things better.

If this intuition and nurturing could be harnessed and applied in the world of work, politics, and social services, we would see a very different world indeed.

A New Perspective

Our world needs this perspective now. We have pushed the get-ahead mentality to the brink of disaster. We need to turn our affairs toward a direction of greater compassion and friendliness if there is to be any hope for peace and prosperity.

We have allowed our nation to pollute the earth. We have allowed abuse to flourish in our homes, offices, and institutions. We

> *W*e need to turn our affairs toward a direction of greater compassion and friendliness if there is to be any hope for peace and prosperity.

have witnessed the presence of bigotry in various forms without doing anything about it. We have given power to those who take it without questioning their authority. As we watch our society struggle with current social and economic issues, we have to acknowledge that old ways may be dying to allow new ways to flourish.

The rebellious youth of the 60's began stirring things up with questions. This questioning has filtered into the foundation of our society. We have been shocked by lies

and cover-ups in government. Racial hatred is alive and well in every town. Sexual abuse occurs in ordinary, upstanding households. Harassment exists throughout our working world yet is denied by the perpetrators. Addictions help people cope in the majority of our households.

We are now willing to look at the underbelly of our world. Much of what we see, we don't like. It has caused us to question the material values we pursued so wildly because so many have been left behind. Clearly, we want a new model.

From The Ground Up

We can look to what happens in therapy for our clues. When a person begins therapy, she finds that in order to get better, she must feel worse for awhile. She has to face the inner pain she has tried so hard to cover up with food, work, alcohol, drugs, sex, and so on.

As she examines her real feelings and where they came from, all of her illusions about her life crumble into pieces. Her childhood wasn't as perfect as she thought it was. Her parents did not recognize her real needs. She learned to use food to anesthetize the pain. Her inner esteem was shattered into small, incoherent pieces. And finally, she uncovered the deepest memories—she was abused and the perpetrator was never caught.

When the truth is out, she begins the tedious, overwhelming, and ultimately exciting process of rebuilding her life. From the very ground up, she chooses which of her values stay and which do not. Which behaviors stay and which do not. Which people stay and which do not. What lifestyle choices are appropriate and which are not.

Slowly, the structure of her new life gets built, piece by piece. She continues to work hard at saying "yes" to healthy things and "no" to unhealthy choices. As her power and strength increase with every new choice, her life begins to flourish again according to values she can really believe in.

Truth Uncovered

This is what is happening in our world. In the last 30 years, we have seen the uncovering of dark social secrets. We have more to find out. But the trend is in motion, and no one wants to turn it off. However painful it is to find out that spiritual leaders misuse their power and abuse children or that one out of four women are sexually abused, we are finally getting free from the secret pain that is created when truth is covered over.

However difficult personal change is, doing it collectively with a nation or world of peoples is almost inconceivable. Yet change occurs regardless. Too often, it has taken a disaster in human history to finally motivate real change. We just get too comfortable: *"We'll try to change it tomorrow. What can we really do anyway?"* So the trends continue until a health epidemic or natural or economic disaster forces the old way out.

Women As Leaders

In this time of revolutionary change, women are leading the way. The majority of people in therapy are women. Women are more often courageous enough to feel their feelings, know that they have to come to terms with their shortcomings and pain, and find better alternatives. Men are often too

frightened of the dark emotional turmoil they find within themselves because the destructive potential is so great. However, as they open up and embrace their pain, this destruction is converted into compassion and new understandings.

Perhaps it is no coincidence then that women are also leading the way into political and economic change. An unprecedented number of women were voted into office this past year. More than half the new businesses that are started are started by women. Women are taking their personal questioning and change and saying the old way is not good enough. It too often does not support values of nurturing and compassion which are so central to the lives of women.

As we take on the task of personal and social change, we are learning how little we know about true nurturing. For example, we often do not extend compassion to ourselves. When our hearts are in pain, we use food to soothe our feelings, hoping to create a foundation of well-being. But it simply does not work in the long run. We find that out very quickly. Part of our task then is to learn ways to nurture ourselves that are more respectful, honest, and accepting. Then our gifts to the world will be more constructive.

Loving Myself

have been living with you, my dear self a long time now. We have been through a lot together. I have learned to listen to you in ways I never knew were important before. I have heard you cry. I have heard your anger. Most of all, I have heard how alone you have felt all these years.

You have been faithful to me. You have never left me. Whatever I do to you or to others, you are always there. However horrible my thoughts are, you are always there. However low my spirits get, you are always there. From you, I learn about loyalty, steadfastness, faith, and hope. From you, I learn that anything is possible. I learn to dream.

Long ago, I came into this world and found it was harsh and confusing. I did not feel welcomed. I did not feel like I belonged. I made my way by following rules and keeping quiet. This got me places, but it really got me nothing.

One day, you woke me up. I turned inside and found a whole new world to explore. I was excited to learn that I could be more me. It took awhile to figure out that meant learning to hurt. I had already spent so much of my time blocking out pain. But you showed me I had to find the hurt, listen to it, accept that it was really there and why, learn to understand it, and then grow beyond it. That was hard.

Now I'm quite good at finding old pain and letting go of it. I have dared do it enough times that I know I'll feel better afterward. I do not balk at facing your feelings anymore.

Yet my growing courage and commitment are not enough. I find something is missing. I do not feel the love I want to feel. I wonder if I am not cut out to love. I wonder if I am crippled in some way that will not let me really get love right.

I want too much from a lover. I want the world to parent me. I want everyone to know and understand what I am going through. I must want too much from love.

So I ask you to teach me once again. Please show me where I've gone wrong. How has my thinking gotten twisted? Why is my heart so wounded? What can I do to repair myself?

You take me gently by the hand and lead me inward. I listen to old feelings. I remain aware of how hidden gifts of insight can come in a flash from picking up the right book, hearing the right comment, meeting the right person just when you need it. But nothing comes.

I feel alone. Abandoned. This is not something someone else can fix. Love springs from inside, but my light has gone out.

Out of the blue come two calls. One caller is afraid of relationships. He won't let me in to do the job he wants me to do. I can feel how bruised he is and the remarkable defenses he puts up. He will never receive anything until he lets down the fence.

The other caller is a man who dares to love. He inspires me to reach inside again and love myself. He reminds me that love is all there is. He asks me to fall in love with myself.

Something suddenly clicks. I realize my fences are just as high as the first caller's. I have not let love in because I was afraid. I have not even let in my own love because

I shielded myself so well. I had learned to care, nurture, and listen, but not to love.

Now I am learning to fall in love with myself. I ask myself throughout the day: *what would be the loving thing to do for you now*? I always get an answer. I am calmer. I feel fuller. I feel surrounded by love, and it all comes through me. I have let down the fence so that love can begin flowing. I focus only on myself. It is all I can do.

I am gentler now. I take time to do what is important. I sleep and eat better. I work with less frenzy. I worry less. I am more willing to trust. I am more present in this very moment, and so is love.

Once again, I have turned my self inward and heard an inner wisdom. There are always answers in the deep, silent self. I only have to ask. Sometimes it takes time for the answers to come. I suspect the answers are there all along, but I have to be ready to hear them. For this lesson, I am grateful. I needed to feel the grace and gentility that comes with loving attention. I can now give it to myself.

As I live this way and radiate who I am, I affect those around me more positively. I still do not fully understand my relationships with others...but I have my self back.

As I express this most simple and elementary love, I feel the universe move through me. The love feels bigger than my self. The teacher feels bigger than my self. I do not really know where the insight comes from, but I know that if I turn inward, the truth will always be there.

The Search for Love

Why is it that we are always looking for love? Unless we are in the exhilarating first stages of new love, many of us are unsatisfied with the relationships in our lives. Relationships seem to be something in which we are often not very skilled or successful.

It used to be that people accepted the families they were in, the spouses they had, the friends they knew, and the town they grew up in. But today, we seek for true happiness in every area of our lives.

This is a laudable goal. There is no reason not to want the best in every way. But there is a real problem with the way we go about trying to get the best.

Blaming Others

Most of us find fault with the situations we are in and blame others or circumstances for causing things to go wrong. So we go

What is the reality of a relationship? It is conscious and careful sharing. It is communication about our needs, hopes, fears, and desires. This kind of communication cannot be done casually. It takes hard work and honesty.

looking for new people and new settings thinking that somehow, we will find the ideal combination.

We are usually looking in the wrong direction. What we are really looking for is a feeling of wholeness, contentment, love, warmth, and so on. We think that other people are the cause of those missing feelings. They are not. We are the only ones who can give ourselves those feelings by loving and accepting ourselves first.

When we are in love, we love how we feel. We not only love the other person, but we love ourselves more. When we are in love, the whole world seems softer and more lovable.

Filled With Love

It is because we are filled with the feelings of love. The other person did not give us those feelings, he or she was just the stimulus for them. They are really happening inside of us.

If you notice, having a wonderful time at the movies or a picnic make you feel happy and full, too. That feeling of joy bubbling up can come from many kinds of stimulation. It just so happens that the intensity of being in love prolongs these feelings for a few days or even months before the everyday reality sets in.

What is the reality of a relationship? It is conscious and careful sharing. It is ongoing communication about our needs, hopes, fears, and desires. This kind of communication cannot be done casually. It takes hard work and honesty. Most of us have had too few models for this kind of love. Our parents and other adults probably did not provide good examples. And we have not had much practice ourselves. So we are not very good at it.

Being Honest

We are not very good at being honest because we are scared that we will lose the person. We are not very good at expressing our needs constructively; too often, we do not even know what we need. We may wait until we are very upset, and then cause a scene. We are also reluctant to share our desires and dreams because we are not sure that we deserve having them fulfilled.

This means that there is a lot we do ourselves in relationships which causes things to turn sour. We intend for everything to be wonderful, but we are not able to pull it off.

To change this pattern, we need to recognize that since feelings of love come from within, anything that stimulates a joyful, more loving feeling inside us benefits ourselves and our relationships. Adding these elements enriches our relationships.

Also, by patiently and diligently developing our relationship skills and committing to our own growth, we can in turn improve our connections with the important people in our lives.

Exercise: *Make a list of the qualities you like in someone you love. You can do this for a lover and for a friend. Think of as many words to describe what is important to you as possible.*

Now rate yourself on each of these qualities (from 1 to 10 with 10 being the best). Notice which are your own strengths. Are there areas in which you could improve? What could you do to strengthen those qualities?

Make another list that describes the kind of lover or friend you usually attract. Again, use as many word as possible. Try and list both positive and bothersome qualities.

Once again, rate yourself on each of these qualities. Look especially hard at the negative ones. Are there any clues for you in your answers? Is there a repeat pattern in other people's behavior to you that you do not like? Why are you attracting this kind of person? These are very big questions which usually take a long time to sort out.

If we have set up a pattern of someone not paying enough attention to us, for example, it may take several situations with several people before we notice the similarity. Once we notice it, we have to ask ourselves why we are attracted to that kind of person and why that kind of person likes us.

After much personal insight, we might finally realize that we feel that we do not actually deserve any more attention than that because that is all we ever got from the time we were little. It may have been that we grew up in a house where our mothers or fathers did not have the time or the know-how to show us love (many of our parents grew up in situations where they were not very nurtured either).

Making Relationships Work

Wouldn't it be nice if everything went along smoothly and people just loved each other? Instead, relationships are something that we cannot take for granted. We have to work to make them grow.

Real Love

Many of us assume that if people really loved us, they would treat us nicely all of the time and that they would know exactly what we need. We may not say that aloud, but we suffer deeply when people do not give us what we think they should.

We have expectations about how those we know and love should behave toward us and others. If they don't, we consider their behavior rude, inconsiderate, unfeeling, or uncaring. This is especially true when we are the recipient of their actions.

A Self-Centered Approach

If they miss the mark, it can hurt our feelings and make us feel that they don't care enough about us. We assume people who are close to us know—or at least should know— exactly how we feel about things. We assume we have told them or indicated in some way our feelings or needs. Even if we didn't, we think it should be obvious.

These are really very self-centered assumptions. Yet we react from assumptions like this more than we realize.

Growing Relationships

Relationships are very organic processes. Cultivating them is a lot like gardening. If we set out to raise a plant either from seed in a garden or even a small, potted plant, we have just entered into a relationship. Why? Because that plant or seed will require our ongoing attention.

We will have to remember it is there. We will have to extend the effort to check on its well-being. Is it thirsty? Does it look healthy? Will it be hurt by wind, heat, or frost? Do we have to do something to protect it? Would they like to hear some music? (Evidently, plants grow better if they are talked to and if they have soothing music to listen to—just as people do.)

Plants are living beings that need our attention to flourish. So are our friends, lovers, mates, children, and other family members. People are like different kinds of plants. They require different kinds of attention from us to flourish. By noticing how they are and how they respond to our attention, we can learn what works for them.

Creative Attention

This takes creativity on our part. We tend to get into ruts and do the same old thing with the same person until we are both bored. Then we wonder what went wrong. Love is not habit. Love does not feel good if we do something just because it is what we have always done or what people expect.

That means we have to work to keep things fresh and alive. We have to share new thoughts and ideas, try doing new things together, meet new people together, or add surprises to a routine.

People Love Surprises

Getting a surprise means someone went out of their way to think of something nice to do for another. This can really touch someone's heart. It can be as simple as buying one flower or doing a favor for others. If they are not good at saying "thank you" out loud, make sure to notice their reaction. They may simply be shocked that someone bothered to do something so nice for them. It is surprising how much we all suffer from low self-image: it is often hard to recognize and accept acts of kindness or love because they are so infrequent.

Wounded Selves

Most of us have self-esteem that has been wounded by hurtful and unloving events throughout our lives. We have come to expect that we will not get the love we want or treatment we deserve. We think that somehow we must not really be worth it, or we would feel better about things.

So when someone does something nice, it catches us by surprise. We are almost a little scared to react: we don't want to scare the person off and we don't want to let ourselves think this is how it really should be in case it does not last. We are really very tender and fragile inside.

Tender Needs

We are like plants, too. We require attention, care, nurturing, and protection on a regular basis from those we love. If we are not getting it, what can we do?

The most obvious answer is to make sure we have relationships with those who want to be "gardeners." If our friends or partners are people who are not really interested in cultivating relationships, then they will not dedicate the time or effort to see how we are and respond to our needs.

It is very difficult to make others love us. Or to change them into something that he or she doesn't want to be. If we find ourselves in unloving or unsatisfying relationships, we may need to consider looking elsewhere to get our needs met. Otherwise, we will always feel like we are starving.

Emotional Starvation

This feeling of starving for attention in relationships is often one of the underlying reasons for unhealthy eating patterns. We know we are not getting nourishment, so we try and feed ourselves. The thing is, food feeds only our bodies—not our hearts.

Since we may have been feeling a lack of attention since we were very little, it may be a very little child inside of us that keeps making the decision to eat. She just isn't grown up enough to know that food will not fix what is making her hurt.

We have to work very hard as adults to recognize these patterns, accept the feelings we have of being lost and unloved, and then begin to figure out how to do it differently. This is really the work of therapy or honest inner personal dialogue.

New Skills

We also need to make sure the people with whom we have key relationships are skilled or not. If the person wants to be a companion but is scattered, he or she may forget to check in with us. If they check but don't know how to tell what we are feeling, then our needs will not be met.

Our friends, families, or partners need to take time to be with us and listen. Even if they do, if they simply cannot hear us or understand our communication, we may end up frustrated anyway.

There is no sense in blaming other people for not knowing something—they simply do not know. Then we must identify if they are willing to learn. We can talk things through with them, or make suggestions in a way that inspires them to try instead of dampening their spirit with criticism.

We have to tell them how much we appreciate them and how valuable the relationship is. Then we must let them know how much we want the relationship to grow. We can say that we have not had much practice at asking for things we need, but we would like to learn together. Then we must see what their reaction is.

Connecting & Communicating

This conversation will only be the very first of many, many more. Once we begin the process of communicating our needs, we will find things changing only if we commit to having them change. This means we have to put energy into having it grow. We get our needs met by nurturing the relationship, too.

Admittedly, we might prefer not having to do all of this. It would be much easier if others were psychic enough to know all of our needs! But most people aren't. Besides, as we change, our needs change. If the relationship stayed the same, we would outgrow it or be bored. It actually is more satisfying in the long-run to be in a relationship where people are openly communicating even if it takes more work.

Alert At The Wheel

We tend to think that once we asked for something, that should be enough. But that is like thinking that if we turn on the car it should be enough to get us where we want to go. Rather, we need to very carefully give it gas, steer it in the direction we want, manage to turn at the right point, and slow down when there are things in the way.

We have had to learn all of these steps of driving and monitoring road conditions and traffic all while continually checking to see that we are on the right route. We have practiced these skills again and again each time we drive. Somehow we think that we do not need to do all of this with our relationships—that they should come naturally and easily to us.

Once we start a relationship growing or changing we need to "stay alert at the wheel." We need to check what is happening in the surroundings, because life stresses will cause "accidents" which might keep us from getting where we are going. We need to keep checking whether we are on the right "road" or not. Are we going in a direction that is making us happy or that is getting us where we want to go?

Committing Ourselves

Without a doubt, relationships take a lot of work—perhaps more than anything else in our lives. That is because they are always changing. Since both people grow and

change, the relationship inevitably will change. There is nothing to do about it except learn to enjoy its evolution and participate in the process. If indeed relationships are like gardening, we can take heart. Throughout the year, gardens grow and become beautiful. They weather the changing seasons, and continue to bloom year after year with kind and patient attention.

As we learn to listen kindly to the needs of others, we learn to also listen to our own needs. As we get stronger and able to ask for more of what we need, we are often able to give ourselves more what we need, too. We bloom from both inside and out, getting the nourishment we need from ourselves and others. Relationships are a two-way partnership. We need to make sure we are playing our part.

Exercise: *Go to a gardening store and buy some empty pots, potting soil, and some seeds. Follow the directions, and plant your seeds. Everyday, watch them grow. Check how they are doing. Talk to them. Notice how much patience it take to watch them come to life. It seems to take forever.*

Watch how delighted you are when you see the first sprout or a new leaf. See how proud you are when it begins to resemble a full-grown plant. Think about what you want to do with it—keep it inside, transfer it outside, etc.

Now, try and recognize these same stages in every relationship. Something is always sprouting! It is probably good to keep a few plants on hand to remind us of how things grow.

The Blessing of Friendship

Most relationships come and go in our lives. Very few relationships are eternal. Perhaps blood relatives come the closest because we always have a bond of some sort.

Friends, on the other hand, are often circumstantial. That is, we meet them because they are in the same class, live in the same building, work in the same place, or are in the same group. This means that when our circumstances change, often our friends change, too.

Different Strengths

For some people, having changing sets of friends is an ordinary experience. Someone who moved a lot as a child gets used to meeting new friends every year. If a person changes schools, jobs, or takes up new interests frequently, this also creates the opportunity to meet new people.

Other people come from very stable backgrounds. They grow up in one small town or neighborhood, playing with the same kids year after year. They stay at the same job and in the same home for years. This gives them a much more stable set of friends over time.

Learning To Change

There are advantages and disadvantages to both ways of living. A person who moves and changes a lot may become very good at adapting to new circumstances and meeting new people. She develops the confidence and trust in herself to handle new things. She knows she can make a place for herself among new people.

On the other hand, she may feel like she has no one other than herself that she can really count on. She is without roots. This may leave her fragile and very vulnerable. She may put up protective defenses in her new, alien situation which prevent her from developing true, intimate relationships. She does not have old, best friends to turn to for sharing her troubles or feelings.

She can—if she puts energy into it—find new people to connect with and develop very special relationships by choice even if her life keeps changing. These new relationships can become very deep. With attention, friendships that develop due to shared circumstances rather than history can be strong and last a very long time.

Solid Base

The person who stays put throughout her life has roots. She knows where she come from and who her people are. There is a continuity to her life that enables her to

The support of good, close friends is one of the most valuable resources we can have to get us through life.

count on others being there tomorrow for her. She has people she can call true friends.

On the other hand, she may be afraid of new situations and relationships because she has not had much practice. Everything and everyone different seems forbidding and frightening. Her world is narrow. She has not gained the confidence to explore new possibilities.

The person whose circumstances stay the same may stick with the same friends simply because they are familiar—even if they do not share her interests any longer or support her changing in any way.

Familiar can be comforting. It can also feel safe. While it may hold her back from venturing into new experiences, it could also give her the security to step out and explore new interests. If she has something to come home to, then she may dare to experiment by meeting new people or trying new things. In the best of all worlds, she may end up with a combination of old friends and new friends.

Finding a Friend

If somewhere on the path of personal encounters in our lives we happen to develop close relationships, then we are indeed lucky.

A deep or "best" friend is one of the most special relationships each of us will ever have. It can be one of the most intimate and one of the most trustworthy relationships we ever experience. It is something to develop, work on, and keep. Too often, especially with busy lives, we do not take time to share our real feelings. Sharing—real, honest sharing—deepens relationships. But sharing is not done on the run. We have to make time for it.

We also have to be willing to take the risk to open up and talk about what is really happening to us. This creates a special bond that may not be as old as family, but it may run as deep. Nurture it. Treat it as if it were gold.

The support of good, close friends is one of the most valuable resources we can have to help us get through life. If we are struggling with hard times, big problems, or eating issues, this kind of support is the foundation to healing and rebuilding what we want for ourselves.

Exercise: *If you are a person who has changed a lot in your life and who knows many different people, then you may find yourself without deep friends you can count on. Pick someone you like for some reason and ask her to lunch or for a walk—some activity during which you will be able to talk.*

If you are a person that has known the same people for most of your life, pick someone you do not know very well and ask her to lunch or for a walk, etc. If you do not know anyone new, take a class or begin a hobby involving other people. Then when you meet someone new that interests you, set up a rendezvous of some sort.

At lunch (or whatever), plan on sharing at least one thing you do not ordinarily tell most people you know. See if she opens back up to you. Let it build, step by step. If you find out that there is really not enough in common to go further with this particular friendship, try the whole thing again with another person.

Our Inner Spirits

" *Developing the strength, vision, courage, or insight we need is a matter of time. We know inside that this is a process, a step-by-step learning process. We are willing to go through it because there is no other choice. It is the nature of life.* "

I Resolve

*I **Resolve*** *to live this year fully, to grow to the best of my capability.*

*I **Resolve*** *to accept my own pace, to know that I step forward slowly, and sometimes even move backwards for a pace or two.*

*I **Resolve*** *to trust my own needs, to know that they guide me and will tell me when I am pushing too hard or when I am doing something to please someone else instead of me.*

*I **Resolve*** *to be kind to myself this year. I know that I need gentleness and acceptance for all of my imperfections as well as my abilities.*

*I **Resolve*** *to be more of me even if others might be surprised. I will let my uniqueness out in little ways whether it be through my words, my appearance, my actions, or my feelings.*

*I **Resolve*** *to pay more attention to my body, to listen when it is hurting, and to try and figure out why.*

*I **Resolve*** *to pay more attention to my feelings, to listen to them when I am hurting and to try and figure out why.*

*I **Resolve*** *to lean on others, to find people I trust even if only a little. This will lighten my load.*

*I **Resolve*** *to remain open to possibilities because life is a surprise. I do not know what is coming. I will rise to meet every challenge and smile at every simple gift life gives me.*

*I **Resolve*** *to hope fiercely for everything I desire. I will keep my dreams alive knowing they lead me into more of me. They give me something to reach for, a purpose.*

*I **Resolve*** *to trust the Universe, the God that made things, the Inner Spirit or Higher Self—I am learning to know there is something bigger than me that I can draw upon for strength and perspective, however I choose to name or describe it.*

Resolve to let go of perfection because I will never succeed. Real perfection is acceptance of the imperfect—knowing it is perfectly fine to be imperfect.

Resolve to honor my life in the highest way possible, to give myself the care I deserve. I will get the rest and exercise I need; I will create time to play; I will avoid overworking and overpleasing; and I will seek out supportive resources to help me as I grow this year.

Resolve to befriend the child in me, to let myself be silly and experimental sometimes. I will keep my eyes open for the magic and wonder that ordinary moments can offer when I least expect it.

Resolve to seek help when I need it, when I am over my head, or hurting from something that might overwhelm me.

Resolve to find others who struggle to grow as I do, to culture their friendship with patience and loyalty.

Resolve to accept that not everyone will understand me or be healthy for me to be around. I may have to say no or disappoint another person, and that may hurt me very much.

Resolve to believe that I deserve to be happy, even if I can't really feel this yet. I will trust it is true.

Resolve to keep learning more about myself, to discover what I feel and need so I can grow. I will seek out whatever books, support groups, therapy, friends, and routines that will help this process. I know it is a process: it will not happen overnight.

Resolve to accept that right now, I use food to help me cope. I know that I am trying to heal my hurts so that food will no longer have to bear the burden of comforting me. I also know that this process will take time. It is alright. This is what my life is really about. I am becoming more of myself.

Our Inner Spirits

There is a quality of wholeness, intelligence, and reverence inside all of us that resonates to the universe. But most of us are out of touch with this side of our personalities. What is this inner spirit? What gifts can it offer us?

Our Wiser Selves

All of our insight and creativity come from a deep part of our being that is beyond words. It is a part of our being that for a short moment, standing in the sun or sitting on a beach feels connected, full, purposeful. It is this part of our being that somehow senses when a friend is going to call. It is this part of our being that smiles at the innocence of children, delights in the painting of an artist, and thrills at the sound of music.

It is also the part of our being that knows we can help ourselves, others, and the world in our own small, simple way. This wiser part of our being refuses to give up on our battle with food and other unhealthy parts of our lives—because it knows that something else is possible.

This deep part of our being is connected to the creative intelligence that organizes the universe. It is beyond words and even beyond experience. It stimulates us to seek out answers and to find the greater meaning of life. Even when we are in the darkest of times, we cannot believe that this is all there is: there must be more, even if we do not know how to find it. That deep, wiser part of us reminds us that there is.

How do we connect with and discover that deeper, quieter, richer, more peaceful part of our being? That has been the quest of all great thinkers, artists, and religious visionaries of all time.

The First Step

The first step is to acknowledge that there is a spiritual side of you. What this means to you and the words that you use to describe this part of yourself may be very different from other people you know.

Some people come to know this part of themselves through their church or religious practice. Others begin to sense this part of themselves in nature or in interactions with other people. Yet others get in touch with it through a love of music, reading, or painting and other arts. Still others seem to experience this side of themselves when they use their bodies in an physical activity such as running or even sex.

Whatever makes us feel more expanded, is something we want to repeat. Often these moments of expansiveness are just that—

> *This wiser part of our being refuses to give up on our battle with food and other unhealthy parts of our lives—because it knows that something else is possible.*

moments. They are sweet, full, and make us feel happier. When they pass, we may feel a loss because we want to feel that way all of the time.

The important thing is not what causes these feelings in you—really anything can—but to allow time to experience these fuller moments. It is not a guarantee that every time we put on special music that we will feel some magic, but we are nourishing our spirit. It is not just our bodies that need nourishment.

We need to build something for our inner spirits into our life schedules—just like we build in sleep and eating time for our bodies, time with friends for our emotions, and time at work for our minds.

When we begin to feed the part of ourselves that is hungry for that connection with our deeper selves, we satisfy some of the hunger we have previously relieved with food. This is a wonderful first step on our journey.

Exercise: One exercise to do with yourself is to track the things that actually give you more of a feeling of peacefulness and connection. Tracking means to notice each experience that makes you feel a little more "you" and what causes it. As you become aware of what is nourishing for your inner spirit, add those practices to your life in some comfortable way.

If you like to sit by a running stream or out under a tree, make sure you do it regularly. If listening to arias or new age music transports you, add a few minutes of listening every day. If an early morning walk starts your day much more peacefully, then get up and go. If you find that a few minutes of reading something reflective or contemplative broadens your perspective, then take a few minutes before sleep or on your lunch hour each day.

A Visit To Nature

If you do not regularly spend quiet time in a natural outdoor environment, you may be missing one of the most healing experiences available to all of us at absolutely no cost.

There is something magical about being in the sun or wind, out under the trees, in the middle of a meadow or stretch of desert, or alongside a lake, stream, or ocean. It is the power of nature.

Natural Environments

Nature is an enormous living system that has evolved and endured through tremendous changes. Most cultures characterize nature with feminine energy because of her ability to adapt and nurture life in a myriad of settings.

If we take time to walk, breath, feel, move, or lay still in an environment where we can sense this gentle power and strength, we learn to listen to the wisdom of a great mother.

Why is earth and nature characterized as mother? Most obviously, the air we breathe and water we drink come from her natural systems. The food we need as fuel also comes from her. Our very lives are really supported because of the earth's natural systems. This is true nurturing.

(Interestingly, the food most often used to binge on is highly processed—no longer in a natural form. Good, healthy whole food seems to feed us in a different way.)

Nature Is Nurturing

By creating a regular time in our routines for getting out into natural environments, we let ourselves directly receive this nurturing energy. It is one place we can receive nurture without any judgement or expectation. Nature simply is. It accepts our presence. It shares its light, color, beauty, and innocence freely with us.

If we take time to notice, we often feel a sense of wonder. Laying in a field and looking at the sky makes us feel bigger, more connected to life. Walking under old trees gives us perspectives on time. Being near mountains or the ocean gives us a sense of the bigger power behind life.

Being out in nature gives us the understanding that there is an orderliness to life. Everything lives in such an interconnected way that it truly is not possible for the world to be a chaotic or random creation. We are part of that system. A member of nature. A citizen of earth.

Natural Inspiration

Being reminded of this grandeur is important when we are struggling to grow and change. It is easy to feel alone and small. Sometimes it seems hard to go on. At these times, it is important to seek inspiration. Nature will do that for us.

Taking time to hear what you are actually feeling about things in a quiet, undisturbed place gives you access to a whole new part of yourself.

It may take a bit of practice learning to be outside by ourselves in relatively undisturbed settings. It is so quiet. Actually, they are filled with sounds of wind, birds, water or grass moving, etc. But if we are used to harsher noises like cars, construction, radios, televisions, crowds of people, phones, and office equipment, being outside will seem dead silent.

This silence may be uncomfortable at first. If we stay for a few moments, we will find that we can listen to our own thoughts, feelings, and wishes. Taking time to hear what we are actually feeling about things in a quiet, undisturbed place gives us access to a whole new part of ourselves.

Natural Therapy

When we become comfortable with our inner quiet selves, we will find that we can go there to find out what is bothering us. It may be easier to do if we are out in nature.

We can each go to that quiet self to talk through problems or gain insight. It is because nature is so huge and patient that we often receive clear understandings there about ourselves if we take the time.

In our modern, hectic world, we have forgotten the value of this great resource to us personally. We have become disconnected. We know we do not like to feel unconnected from important support systems like parents, friends, and community. It is unhealthy.

Is it any wonder that since we are disconnected from a daily experience of nature that we no longer feel part of a larger whole, that the magic of life seems gone?

We can remedy that situation ourselves by spending time outside in natural environments, especially those that have not been radically changed by humans. We may have to travel a bit to do it, but it is worth the effort. If we let the clean, open, simple majesty of our earth and her many special places into our experience, our inner spirits will grow in health, hope, and happiness.

Exercise: *Find a spot in nature that you like. Travel a bit if you have to. It is worth taking a few hours or a day. Find a place to sit or lie down that feels peaceful to you.*

Settle in and let yourself get quiet. Notice everything around you. Notice the clouds moving by. Notice the light on the leaves. Notice the ants hurrying home. Notice the buzzing of bees or the smell of damp earth. Let your senses take in the smells, sounds, and sensations of these lovely surroundings. Notice how simple it all is. Notice how well all the parts seem to work together.

Close your eyes and continue to feel the sensations of your surroundings. Let yourself relax into the peacefullness of the day. If feelings and thoughts come up about your life, let them surface. Talk them over with yourself. Pretend nature is listening. Ask for advice. What would she say if she could help?

If insights come, don't be surprised. In places like these, creativity and wisdom is often enhanced. Thank yourself, the day, and nature for the experience. Come back again as soon as you like.

Hope: The Doorway To The Future

Very few people get to go through life smoothly and without troubles. It almost seems as if we are given challenging circumstances to develop our abilities and to grow stronger as people.

When we are in the middle of the struggle, the world gets very dark. We have no idea how we are going to get out of this. It is not easy living in darkness. The human spirit can withstand very tough ordeals, but not without hope. No one lasts very long without hope.

Reason To Believe

Hope is the central ingredient to recovery from an eating disorder, addiction, illness, financial crisis, or emotional strain like divorce or breaking up with a partner. Why?

Hope gives us vision. It gives us reason to believe that things will move on and change. We can trust that we will one day feel less overwhelmed by these circumstances.

Hope, belief, and trust are qualities of the spirit. They are hard to prove. They are easy to ridicule. But they are the backbone of our personal growth.

Hope is not unreasonable. It is not unreasonable to think things will change. Things always change. No day is like another. We are not the same people we were five years ago.

It is impossible that we will get stuck in one spot forever. That is why we hope. We know inside that we change. We just don't know how long it will take to get through this phase.

We wonder how long we are going to feel so overwhelmed, and when we will feel strong enough to handle this challenge. We want to know how fast we can grow.

No one can answer that. That is where trust enters in. We find ourselves willing to hope because we trust the fact that we are learning and growing just a bit every single day.

A Personal Journey

This process of hoping, trusting, and growing builds our faith. We develop faith in our ability to change, in the purpose of the process, and in life itself. Getting through hard times is what builds that faith.

Each person pulls upon different resources as she copes with this growing process. A special friend, a religious practice, family members, meaningful work, or a morning run might make the transition a little easier. Some people turn inward keeping a journal or working with a therapist. Some find support groups helpful.

> *The human spirit can withstand very tough ordeals, but not without hope. No one lasts very long without hope.*

Developing the strength, vision, courage, or insight we need is a matter of time. We know inside that this is a process, a step-by-step learning process. We are willing to go through it because there is no other choice. It is the nature of life.

In the end, we can look back and see how far we have come. We can see the challenges we faced and how much they made us grow. We know there will be others ahead. It is the way things go. It makes us stronger and deeper people.

In Praise Of Selfishness

At some point in our growth toward becoming full human beings, we have to learn to be selfish and self-centered. This may sound strange because all of our lives we have been taught to be kind and courteous—to put others' needs in front of our own.

This is more true for females than males since women are most often the emotional glue in personal and family relationships.

If The Shoe Fits

Saintly behavior is admirable if the shoe fits, but devastating if it doesn't. If we have become unique, strong, and deeply self-assured individuals who choose to give to others out of strength, then we are a joy to be around.

> *If one of the things we want to do in life is to help others or to make others feel good, then it is important to recognize that we can give only to the extent of our personal strength.*

This kind of giving is rare because very few people have taken the time to focus on themselves for extended periods until they have such strong centered beings that they can let go and give just for the sake of giving.

Most of us want something in return—and others feel it. We want to be noticed and thanked for our efforts. We want to be praised for the giving we do.

No Free Lunch

In other words, our giving has a price tag. This can make our friends, children, coworkers, and mates feel resentful of our tainted giving and drive them away. We are left feeling confused and unappreciated.

In reality, we are using others to feel good about ourselves. We see ourselves as good because we give. But we give to feel good about ourselves! People resent being used. They can sense when we need them to tell us we are wonderful.

A Personal Focus

Our relationships will become richer and less troubled, and we will feel better about ourselves if we take the time to focus on our own development before or in addition to doing things for others. Then we will truly be strong enough to choose to give for the sake of giving.

Is this selfish? Yes, but the purpose is pure. If one of the things we want to do in life is to help others or to make others feel good, then it is important to recognize that we can give only to the extent of our personal strength.

Helping Ourselves

If we give and we do not need to have someone notice or commend us, then we have enough personal strength to know that we are worthy people regardless of what others think. There is a freedom in this that makes giving a pleasure for its own sake.

Taking time to focus on growth even if we have responsibilities to families or other people will be more rewarding for them as well as for us.

Handling The Blues

Some days are harder than others to get through. We don't feel good. Our bodies ache and are slower than usual. Our minds are dull, and there is heavy pounding inside our brains. Our good will is dampened, and it is hard to be positive about anything. It is hard to see past today and know tomorrow will be different.

No one likes to talk about these days. We cry easily and feel sorry for ourselves. Anything can set us off. We feel stuck in situations that are hard to cope with. We don't know where to turn, because we don't know anyone who wants to hear this pain.

Most people know the patient, smiling, positive, friendly, and helpful sides of us. The dark, gloomy, negative, angry, scared, and overwhelmed sides are kept private. We learned early that most people do not like unhappy friends.

A Low Profile

We work hard to be the kind of person others expect us to be. After all, we really like it better when we are happy, too.

But almost all of us have days when we feel down. We cannot ignore the blues, and nothing we do seems to change them. In fact, the harder we try, the more moody we get. We need to handle ourselves gently, lovingly, and with great patience instead.

These are not days to make big decisions or discuss delicate matters. These are the days to keep a low profile and deal with big issues later.

Healing Strategies

There are important findings in the treatment of depression that we can use for our own care on blue days.

Exercise has been found to have a remarkable healing effect. Animals also have an amazing effect on depression by getting our minds off our own troubles for a few minutes and helping us relax.

Light therapy is also proving to be helpful to people who feel depressed during winter seasons and rainy days. Their bodies actually require more light.

The self-help movement has shown millions of people how powerful it is to gather

We cannot ignore the blues, and nothing we do seems to change them. In fact, the harder we try, the more moody we get. We need to handle ourselves gently, lovingly, and with great patience instead.

together with others for support. It is not necessary to talk, just to be there.

Also, as we learn more about the body's chemistry, we find out that mood and nutrition are connected. If we stop eating, binge, or eat nutritionally inadequate foods when we have the blues, we feel much worse because our blood sugar is out of balance and toxins build up.

This is the time to make sure we get protein and complex carbohydrates like whole wheat or fresh fruits and vegetables even though chocolate seems much more comforting.

Stress management techniques help, too, such as playing music, calling a friend, keeping a journal, practicing Transcendental Meditation—whatever works.

55

Finally, if the blues are chronic or related to a painful event(s) now or in the past, we may find therapy is most helpful.

Nothing Is Forever

Luckily, life ebbs and flows. The blues do not stay around forever, particularly if we work hard to be patient and nurture ourselves on these especially tough days.

It is natural to feel down at times. Healthy humans grieve when things aren't right rather than stuff feelings inside. By continuing our commitment to healing ourselves, a blue day or period becomes a step on our paths to wholeness.

Exercise:

On blue days try:

1. Get out and move. Take a simple walk, bike ride, or swim to prevent feelings from getting stuck.

2. Go to a pet store, petting zoo, or take a friend's dog for a walk.

3. Get outside on a daily basis, even if it is only for a 15-minute stroll at lunch.

4. Find a support group or special interest group and make sure you go. You will be tempted to skip days when you need it the most.

5. Try to find a counselor with whom you are comfortable and begin therapy.

6. Buy a full spectrum light bulb and sit under it for 20 minutes or more each day during winter months and rainy or blue days.

Weathering Our Storms

he rains of late spring fill rivers and streams and teach us a lesson in survival.

Heavy rains cause the rivers to swell. The waters swirl with power and disturb the normally quiet bottom. Stirred-up silt turns the water brown and dirty. Tree roots and leaves, garbage, and other debris is dragged into the swift currents.

Flood Of Feelings

We, too, must weather storms. They often release a flood of feelings, memories, and pain from the bottoms of our souls. These feelings usually lie quietly buried under normal activity.

However, great events of our lives have a way of generating so much reaction and change that feelings surface from the very force of that change. Like rivers, we get muddy, too. Feelings flood up, swirl around, gather power, and color our normal, everyday world.

After The Storm

When the waters subside, the rivers resume their normal patterns. There is very little sign that there ever was a storm. A close look reveals an uprooted tree lodged in a new place or newly exposed soil on the banks.

The high waters fed grasses on the river bank and cut new pathways for the water to flow. Floating seeds found new places to root. Old and weaker elements were destroyed, making room for the new. Unwanted debris was carried away.

A Delicate Beginning

Like the river, we get on with our lives after a crisis, but we are never quite the same inside.

Like rivers, we get muddy, too. Feelings flood up, swirl around, gather power, and color our normal, everyday world.

The bottom has been disturbed, and we have had a chance to clean out old feelings and begin new patterns.

For awhile, we may feel tender and unstable until everything settles. Our lives eventually take on a normal rhythm again, quietly flowing until the next storm hits.

Exercise:

After a storm, find a stream or river and pick a comfortable place to observe it for 20 minutes— sit or walk alongside or stand on a bridge.

Look at the waters. Note how swiftly they move, finding a way around every obstacle and taking loose debris along. Can you see the bottom? What is happening at the edges? Notice how the water runs, finding a path. Observe how the banks hold the swell and the clutter is cleaned out.

Remember how everything looked before the storm. Come back a few days later and look again. Remember this for your own storms. You will be able to handle the feelings. The crisis will subside, and you'll feel cleaner.

Big Girls Don't Cry

*L*ittle girls learn early that people won't like them as much if they are not happy. They are told that anger and sadness are emotions they shouldn't feel if they want people to like them. As they grow up, they hear again and again: big girls don't cry.

But big girls do get sad. They do feel anger, fear, confusion, and sorrow. They never learn to express these feelings because other people don't know how to handle them. Family members and others pull away from any unhappiness.

Going Numb

Feelings don't go away, they just go inside. Young girls learn to stuff fear, anger, sadness,

> *W*hen a person begins to heal herself, feeling feelings is always part of the process. She can never be whole until every part of her is alive again.

and rage inside, pretending it is not there. They deny that these emotions even exist.

Eventually, they no longer know when they are feeling sad or angry because "unattractive" emotions are automatically repressed. Part of them goes numb.

On The Move

To get unfrozen, feelings have to move again. They have to be felt. When a person begins to heal herself, feeling feelings is always part of the process. She can never be whole until every part of her is alive again.

It is scary at the beginning because expressing sadness or anger has always meant rejection. People leave if we are sad or mad.

Expressing negative feelings does mean that we risk some people pulling away. We must practice ways to express feelings constructively and honestly in therapy or assertiveness and communication workshops.

Alive and Whole

Letting this real and sensitive side of us out of hiding is very liberating. It will make us feel more alive and whole.

It is also very good for self-esteem. When a part of the self is cut off and kept in darkness, it feels punished or disowned: *Bad things or bad people are kept locked up. So if feelings are bad, and if I have them, then aren't I bad for having them?* When these exiled parts are allowed back in, it sends a signal that this part is acceptable, too.

Big girls do cry, and it feels good. This is the amazing part. We know the therapeutic value of a good cry. Letting ourselves be sad, angry, scared, confused, exhausted, preoccupied, or selfish is just as refreshing.

Each one of these feelings has a purpose. It sends a message to us about how we are affected by the events in our lives. They are actually educational. By listening to them, we learn more about who we are and what is important to us.

Exercise: Sign up for an assertiveness training or communications class to practice telling people what you feel.

Does It Really Matter?

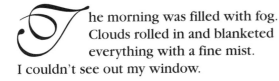

The morning was filled with fog. Clouds rolled in and blanketed everything with a fine mist. I couldn't see out my window.

My head was filled with fog, too. I couldn't get out of bed. I could barely move.

It had been this way for days. I waited for motivation to enter my veins and help me rise up ready for anything. But it never came.

Eventually, slowly, I got up. I wandered about not knowing what to do. I had no list to accomplish. No priorities guided my actions. Even desire eluded me.

The fog moved in closer. I now felt very alone. It was dark even in the middle of the day. What shall I do? Where shall I go? Does it matter?

The Foggy Gift

When personal fog blankets our souls and makes us pull inward, we finally begin asking questions: *Where are we going? Why? Does it really matter?*

Yes, it really matters. No one else lives this life for us. No one else gives us meaning, hope, or purpose.

On foggy days, these ideals seem too lofty. Our heads are buried in muddy soup, so we settle for less. But we feel it. Our lives seem less important. We feel disposable, forgettable. We stop listening. Our feelings get ignored. Our ideas and dreams are no longer heard. Our soul dies, and we wonder what we are living for.

It Really Matters

Yes, it really matters. It matters that we live with quality. It matters that we care—about ourselves, our lives, our energy, our dreams, and the contribution that we make to this small earth.

It doesn't matter how big our lives are. It simply matters how we live. All we can do is decide how to live with quality: what is worth doing to us.

Keeping Small

We start small. Very small. We act with care for ourselves. We keep clean. We brush our teeth. We sleep. We feed ourselves when we are hungry. We dress with care. We keep our homes and cars neat. We go outside to get fresh air regularly.

These simple things give dignity to our lives. We demonstrate to ourselves that we deserve to be treated with respect and loving attention.

Doing simple things with care and responsibility is like pulling weeds. Flowers cannot grow if they are choked out by weeds. It's the same with us. If we forget about the basics, the rest of our lives cannot blossom.

New Seeds

The garden is now ready for planting. What would you like to grow? How would you like to invest your time and energy? How would you like to use your mind and heart? What is interesting? What is worth doing?

There is no ready made set of answers to this question. Our parents have their answers. Our friends have theirs. Our teachers have others. But we have to make answers for ourselves.

No one else can know what really interests our hearts and minds. No one else can guess at our personal motivations. No one else can dictate what will stimulate, excite, or teach us.

Learning To Dream

When we first ask the question, *"what is worth doing?,"* we do not know the answer. We have to answer it by listening to ourselves and then by trying different possibilities.

Some of us are blessed with dreams that are clear from the start: *I want to dance. I want to write. I want to heal people.* These desires drive their decisions. But many of us don't know our dreams. We may not even know what interests us anymore.

We are like little children finding out about the world and ourselves. We watch people. We read about what they do. We learn from television, magazines, and books.

Commitment To Care

We admire those who are committed to whatever they do. They do it well, and they do it from the heart. They do it for pleasure—not for reward.

Whether they work with children, run farms, hand paint cards, volunteer in soup kitchens, or grow window sill gardens—what matters is that they care.

We Become The Nurturers

When someone cares about something, the object of attention automatically becomes important. They care enough to notice. They take time. They spend energy on this person or project. They use thought and creativity.

Whoever or whatever receives this attention is truly nurtured. The person doing the action feels good to have done something, and the recipient benefits from the attention. The action is certainly worth doing. By nurturing something, we nurture ourselves. And creation smiles.

Tossing Out The Old.
Making Room For The New.

As the season changes if you find yourself feeling uncontrollable urges to clean your house, straighten your cupboards, or sort through old clothes, honor these impulses and get moving!

Just as the sap begins to run in early spring waking the trees and causing new buds to form, humans find themselves affected by seasonal changes, too. Days are longer and lighter. When the weather is warmer and more inviting, we want to throw open our windows, let in fresh air, put away old clothes, and clean.

Innocent Impulses

We are renewed by the budding season. If we let ourselves enjoy and express our impulses, we will find ourselves naturally sorting through what is no longer useful to us and starting things new.

The impulse to clean and sort our homes, cars, closets, desks, and purses, is a metaphor for a process that is going on simultaneously on a deeper, more silent level.

Practicing Renewal

We are committed to getting unstuck. We want to live life with more freedom and joy of expression. Therefore, we need to get rid of old baggage that loads us down.

Our need for physical orderliness, cleanliness, and environmental renewal is an important expression of the sorting we are doing on the inside to ready ourselves for new possibilities.

Removing Clutter

It is also an act of respect and love for ourselves. When we walk into a room we have just cleaned, it is easier to sink in and relax. We have made space to "just be" without old clutter. We have taken time to make things feel better.

When we live and work in cleaner, less cluttered spaces, it gives room for our minds and hearts to breathe and heal. Cleaning out our spaces sends a message that our inner work is important to us. Now that we have taken care of the outer clutter, we are ready to turn inward and do the same process of sorting, tossing out the old, and bringing in the new.

Inspiring Energy

We are inspired by our own energy. We really do want to live differently. We are ready to put our commitment into action. We will take the time to examine the old to decide what to keep and what to let go of.

> *The impulse to clean and sort our homes, cars, closets, desks, and purses, is a metaphor for a process that is going on simultaneously on a deeper, more silent level.*

As we change inside, naturally our surroundings will change. What we once could tolerate, we can no longer. We want healthier, cleaner, brighter, more hopeful surroundings, so we go after them with zeal.

Waking Up Inside

Like the trees, we wake up inside. We are done with the quiet darkness. We can no longer hibernate. We must move again. We must change. We must feel alive and do something that makes a difference.

This is a wonderful time to pursue significant changes in our outer lives and in therapy. It is also a wonderful time to pursue small changes at home that make us feel safer, more nurtured, and more whole.

Preparing For Action

We are building nests to hatch new parts of ourselves. Just as birds gather twigs and fuzz to prepare for new little birdlings, we create structures and environments that will give us stability yet be gentle enough to allow us to put our new desires into action.

We have been thinking deeply all winter. Now we want to change. Being comfortable in our surroundings will help us change. It helps us let go of reactions and beliefs that are no longer constructive. It creates an invitation to try something new.

Perhaps it is some old instinct from nature that causes us to sort, toss, and clean. Regardless, it helps prepare us to express new discoveries about ourselves.

Exercise: Even if you do not have an impulse to tear apart your closet or scrub a floor, find a messy corner, drawer, room, file, etc that needs attention. Pick something that you have been putting off doing. Go after it step by step. This may be a project you can do in an hour. It make take all week. If it is really big, you may be working at it for the entire month. Break it apart into achievable goals. As you work, let yourself notice how this feels similar to the personal work you are doing inside to change. As you sort and clean, you may find thoughts and feelings coming up about personal matters you'd like to work on. Use the inspiration to make a difference in your life!

Making Peace With Pain

Whether we like it or not, there is a dark side of life. Some traditions call it evil, some refer to it as a destructive force, and some suggest it exists because humans have denied their true feelings or have not yet developed their full conscious potential.

Whatever the reason and wherever it comes from, we find ourselves face to face with painful experiences that come at the hand of other people.

Abusive Power

From physical and sexual abuse to the misuse of authority to highway carelessness or neighborhood terrorism, humans hurt humans. Whether they are re-enacting painful treatment they received at some earlier time or are acting out of empty and angry souls, they create new wounds for others. This way, pain ripples through layers of society, generation after generation.

Each of us has to come to terms with this dark side of life experience. Some people deny that this negativity exists at all and focus only on the positive. Some get so frightened that they can no longer make any moves in their lives. Others decide that if life has a cruel streak, they don't have to be responsible any longer. They get cynical, cavalier, and even deliberately hurtful.

Darkened Hope

Being on the receiving end of someone senselessly acting out the pain in his or her soul is deeply destructive. It undermines our trust in human nature, God, ourselves, the future, and life on this planet. It can put out the tiny light of hope that burns fiercely in most of us. It can make us wonder if it is worth even living.

When such disturbing events occur in our lives, much of our psychic energy goes into making sense of the trauma. This can take a very long time—years or even a whole lifetime. Until we can come to terms with why pain happens or how it fits into our lives, we are on shaky ground. Our very souls tremble and feel vulnerable.

We need to settle and numb pain periodically just to have a breather, to take a rest from the inner turmoil that is always churning beneath the surface. Food serves this purpose for many of us. We chew ourselves into blankness and stop the awareness of our struggles for just a short time.

The Meaning Of Pain

We hope to escape them altogether, but it never works. Yet somehow, the act of mindlessly chewing, swallowing, reaching, and repeating deadens the inner ache for a short time.

We must eventually find a way to make peace with why pain happens. Many people say they grow from the pain in their lives.

> *Being on the receiving end of someone senselessly acting out the pain in his or her soul is deeply destructive. It undermines our trust in human nature, God, ourselves, the future, and life on this planet.*

Without it, they would not be challenged to question unhealthy patterns, learn about deeper aspects of themselves, and develop new strengths and broader perspectives. In short, pain seems to create wisdom.

Experiencing painful events takes away our arrogance as humans. We like to think we have everything in control. Time and time again, we find that things do not go as we had planned. Our lives veered off in unexpected directions which threw us off kilter for awhile.

Pain also has a way of evening out status. We are always judging ourselves as better or lesser than others based on intelligence, looks, wealth, personality, creativity, or position. Pain is a great equalizer. We come to see that we are all equally capable of wounding. When we hurt, we are not better or worse as people—we just hurt.

Into Our Souls

Perhaps most important, pain takes us into our souls. When we suffer, we re-interpret what is truly important to us. Most find that inner happiness and peace is much more precious than a good salary, bigger title, better grades, or any award. We begin to direct our energies at self-healing instead of focusing solely on worldly pursuits.

This redefinition of priorities is at the core of what people say happens to them when they have to confront real pain. They re-define what it means to be human, what it means to love (oneself and others), and what it means to live. Pain makes us ask about the meaning of life.

Although people describe the meaning of life in dramatically different ways, they all refer to a deeper layer of human life that gives more meaning to daily activities. We often discover this inner core of ourselves— our souls—as we seek to make peace with the pain in our lives.

Dropping Into Silence

Driving away from the city, it becomes apparent how much noise fills our everyday world: racing engines and honking traffic, songs blaring on the radio, people talking to each other, phones ringing, and equipment humming.

Out in the countryside, if we listen, we still hear a great deal: crickets, wind in the grasses, a distant tractor, a plane overhead, and water rippling by in a stream. Yet out here, the decibel level is lower, and we can hear ourselves really think.

Many of us reach for the radio or television when it is too quiet. We have gotten far away from lifestyles which value the integration of silence on a regular basis. Yet we still know how valuable it is.

Heal And Inspire

No symphony is composed without silence to emphasize the sounds that move us. A good storyteller knows how to add important pauses to keep us enthralled. Even a reading of poetry is most powerful when the rhythm includes silence in between the words.

In society, we have places of silent power which touch the souls of those that enter: cathedrals, museums, and libraries. Religious services include moments of silence to encourage us to look inward.

Even in therapy, the therapist knows the value of silence. As her client stumbles across a new memory, interpretation of an event, or thought, she may be moved to silence for some time. The therapist allows, respects, and encourages this.

Every artist or creative person says that inspiration arrives often in silent moments of concentration or private communion with the universe. And, of course, few people are unmoved by the silent grandeur of mountains or beauty of nature.

Resisting Distraction

Obviously, something inside of us responds to silence. It needs silence to thrive. When we add regular doses of silence back into our lives, we find our inner world responding with a greater sense of fullness and connection to the creation that surrounds us.

There is no mistake that all religious practices around the world encourage prayer or meditation. Messages often come to us in that silence. They can be inspiring and help us touch the essence of our lives. They may also take us past our limitations into a deeper layer of ourselves.

> *We may have to get beyond boredom or a sense of agitation before we drop into our deeper selves. We are not used to this inner world.*

We may have to get beyond boredom or a sense of agitation before we drop into our deeper selves. We are not used to this inner world. In fact, we learn to reach for something to stop this inward dive. We often reach for food, cigarettes, or other distractions instead of looking inward. If we do, we will miss moments of personal discovery.

We need silence as much as any artist, writer, musician, or religious person. If we can regularly experience deeper layers of ourselves through experiences of silence, we will be richly rewarded. We must simply take the time.

A Prayer For The New Year

As I make my way this year through my growth, may I always remember to listen to my deepest self. There, I find my truth, however gentle or harsh it may be.

I am grateful for the courage I have had this past year because it has taken me through dark days and long nights. I have come through each difficult period a little more whole and conscious of who I am and where I have come from.

I hear the voices of my grandmothers and ancestors guiding my footsteps. They gave birth to me through my parents who learned their truths and their weaknesses from them. I hold these truths in my heart and still struggle with these weaknesses.

I hope to better my world just a tiny bit as I pass through it. Whether my mark is big or small, I do not yet know. I seek first and foremost to be as true to myself as I can be, and hope that this positively impacts the earth and her peoples.

Most of all, I practice using my voice. This has been the hardest to learn because it requires that I speak only truth. I am not strong enough to dare to say all that I know all of the time. I fear hurting others and being hurt in return. But I know my creativity is harnessed to my self-expression. If I remain mute, I cannot make a contribution of any kind.

I vow to support the people I love. Like a carefully tended garden, I listen to their needs, share my feelings, and watch them grow alongside me. I am no longer sure what to expect from them. I am only just learning what to expect from me.

Last of all, I turn my heart, mind, soul, and body to a perspective larger than mine. I listen, hoping to hear the heartbeat of creation. I wait for the breath of the world on my face each morning to bless me. I puzzle, as always, with the mysteries of why things are as beautifully orchestrated and painfully cruel as they are. With each experience, I get wiser. And with each discovery, I am yet a smaller part of a bigger whole. I only pray that I can remain open to take it all in.

Food & *Feelings*

"If we are open to learning about ourselves, our eating, and the way we live, we will naturally find that we are attracted to new ideas or insights that will be right for us. This process keeps happening, helping us to gently adjust our thinking, reactions, and choices."

Why Do We Eat?

Why do we eat? It is important to ask this question because the answers give us the first clues about breaking the patterns in which we are stuck.

Food Is Fuel

Of course we eat to give our bodies the energy they need to get through the day. Food is fuel. It is like putting gas in our cars.

Quality gas makes our cars run more smoothly. Quality food (fresh, well-prepared, with a balance of nutrients) makes our bodies run more smoothly: we can resist colds, flu, and other illnesses; we have more energy; and we feel better.

But the role of food in most families and cultures is much more meaningful than just simple fuel. It becomes a way of sharing and socializing. Most family or community gatherings, holidays and other special occasions, and get-togethers with friends or lovers involve food.

Food Is Friendship

Why is food so central to our lives? It is certainly a source of pleasure that can be enjoyed by all. Perhaps it dates back to our early ancestors who had to hunt or grow their own food: times of plenty were something to celebrate by the whole family, tribe, or village. Food has been scarce for western peoples as recently as the past World Wars. Food is something that few cultures have had the luxury of taking for granted.

Food Is Optional

In the United States, most of us do take food for granted. There still are many who go hungry due to poverty or other hard times, but mainstream America does not worry about whether there will be food on the table.

This makes food an option. We have the luxury of saying "no." We diet, skip meals, burn off the calories, or even use vomiting or laxatives to get rid of the food. If we did not take food for granted, we would never think of these things.

Food Is Love

Food has another important quality. It takes on an emotional meaning. From our very first experience of eating—being held in someone's arms and receiving a warm, soothing sensation that filled us up—we came to associate food with feeling.

Food meant attention. Food meant caring and nurturing. Food meant we were important enough for someone to meet our needs. Food meant love.

Because we are not aware of the connection with food and feelings, we often eat unconsciously. Whenever we feel lonely, frustrated, scared, or hurt we reach for food.

Soothing Ourselves

This is a very powerful association. It continually gets reinforced throughout our upbringing as small children. When we were hurt or feeling bad, our mothers often comforted us with candy, cookies, or even by preparing a favorite meal. We learned to eat our troubles away. Is it any wonder that we reach for food when we are feeling bad?

Later on, as adolescents and young adults, we experience special birthday meals, dinners on first dates, and office parties honoring special occasions. People continue to show their affection and interest through food. Food becomes intimately connected with the demonstration of love, affection, and worthiness.

Food Is Trouble

There is nothing wrong with this. Preparing, serving, giving, or sharing food is a lovely way to do something special for someone. It is even nice when we turn such affection back on ourselves. But this is where the trouble begins.

Because we are not aware of the connection with food and feelings, we often eat unconsciously. Whenever we feel lonely, frustrated, scared, or hurt, we reach for food.

This pattern gets set up when we are very young, so our emotional eating can also begin at a young age. Many people who struggle with food recall eating in reaction to troubles from the time they were five, nine, 13, etc.

Food Is Attention

When we eat, we are unconsciously trying to give ourselves the attention we need to soothe away bad feelings. Since food got associated with someone comforting us, we unconsciously try to get that experience back again by eating. When the feelings do not go away or they come back, we eat more.

What we forget is that food did not fix everything when we were little either. An important part of the process was being held and being able to talk about what we felt so that the feelings could be aired and maybe even resolved.

Temporary Solution

When our troubles get bigger and more complicated as we grow older, there is a smaller chance that food will successfully soothe us. It works for a moment. But the problems and feelings quickly return.

Our minds and hearts are really asking us to solve these problems at another level. That is why they keep coming back. Our inner selves know that food is not the solution. But until we understand why we reach for food and then develop other ways to cope with the feelings instead, the pattern will continue.

Coping with problems in a healthier way involves really understanding and feeling how each difficulty affects us and what we need to handle its impact on our lives. By examining our reactions, either on our own or with the help of therapists, we can begin to let go of the feelings that come from tough times and find solutions that fit our own unique needs.

This process takes a great deal of courage to begin. Once you begin and feel the change it can create, a sense of hopefulness about the future grows. Freedom from the devastating cycle with food is possible.

Exercise: *Begin to keep a log (written notes) tracking when you reach for food. Notice if you are feeling upset or nervous in any way. Identify as much of what is causing you to turn to food as possible.*

At first, this may be hard to do. Be patient. The reason for your upset may come to you later. It is ok. You are simply beginning to notice how the connection between food and feelings works for you.

Best Friend, Worst Enemy

It is a strange relationship that some of us have with food. Those of us who struggle with compulsive eating, overeating, binging, purging, or restricting, go way beyond what most people do with food. We think it has the power to fix our lives when we escape into eating. Other times, we blame it for ruining our lives and making us unhappy. How does this happen?

From the time we were small babies, we have experienced food as comforting. It settled our hungry stomachs and usually meant someone paid attention to us while we were fed. We often were held closely in someone's arms. Our caretaker looked us lovingly in the eyes and spoke soft, sweet words while we peacefully ate our fill.

Conditioned To Comfort

Food and eating came to have positive, comforting associations from these early experiences. We have been conditioned to think of food as love.

Picture a scientific rat who gets sweet food from a red button and bland food from a green button. The rat will keep pressing the red button long after the sweet food is removed. The rat's response is even more powerful if the food that came from the red button was sometimes sweet and sometimes not. The rat will press much longer once the sweet food is stopped, because he has learned that it is not always consistent— the sweet food might show up if he keeps trying.

We learn the same way. We had some wonderful eating and feeding experiences and some that were probably not so nice. But we want that feeling. So when we need comfort, we once again turn to the substance and behavior that has worked so many times in the past. Since this has been conditioned intermittently over a long time, it is a very hard association to break.

A Dependable Companion

In all of our tough experiences, we continue to reach for food. It is always there when we need it. Food never lets us down. It never talks back or acts up. It never questions or challenges us. It never makes us feel as if we are not good enough. It is a steady, dependable companion.

What more could we ask for in a friend? We want people to talk to, to demonstrate that they care, to be actively interested in us. Food cannot do that. Something is missing. Even so, food often takes away at least some of our pain.

Something Is Missing

So we start eating and keep eating. Sometimes it really seems to work. When it doesn't, we keep eating until we find relief. We want more than we are getting from food, so we eat more to find it.

> *Food never lets us down. It never talks back or acts up. It never questions or challenges us. It never makes us feel as if we are not good enough. It is a steady, dependable companion.*

We don't know what else to do. We get desperate. We really need something and don't know where to turn. So we eat more. Now we are really getting scared. So we eat more. It is getting crazy. We cannot stop. We want more, we need more...and then we finally break down. Our bodies stop us in some way.

Our best friend has turned into our worst enemy. Its friendship is false. It led us on. It made us believe we would feel better. It betrayed us. We feel jilted, abandoned. Worst of all, our hopes are gone.

How could we get ourselves into something like this? We know food cannot really comfort us. We know food doesn't really hurt us. But we give it that power. We are trying to comfort ourselves, but the way we choose only ends up hurting instead of helping.

Growing Up

There is no magic in the world. There is no one thing that will fix the problems we have in some simple way. We are hoping that food will take away our pain. We are looking for other people to rescue us. We really wish something or someone would make it all better.

We have to let go of that wish. We have to realize that it is the little girl in us who needed more than she got. Little girls make wishes. It is their nature. But little girls need to grow up and realize that they are really responsible for taking care of themselves. There are very few white knights in real life.

Our Own Best Friend

Taking care of ourselves is scary at first because we have no confidence that we can do it. What we are really learning to do is to become our own best friend. A best friend is someone who is there to listen, someone who will stand by us through thick and thin, and someone with whom we can play and cry.

We can do that for ourselves. In fact, we have to do it for ourselves before anyone else can really be a true friend. Otherwise, we scare people away because we are too needy.

It is unfair to ask others to make us feel good about our lives. That is a big burden. Friends are there to walk alongside us and keep us company. This is a very important role. But they can't keep us safe or make us feel whole. We have to become whole through our own growth. This is very hard work, but it is well worth the effort. In the end, we come out as people we like, and we feel proud to be who we are. That kind of self-acceptance and self-love is truly satisfying.

Exercise: Set aside a day to spend with yourself doing just what you always really wanted to do. Plan it as if you were making a date with a best friend. Take yourself where you would go with your best friend. Treat yourself to the fun things you would do together.

By practicing this way, you are giving yourself the same respect and attention you would give to someone else. Go shopping, drive to the ocean, take yourself to a movie, lay on a blanket in a park, play your favorite albums, try on your clothes, get an ice cream cone...it doesn't matter. Just treat yourself to a day that is wonderful because it is full of the things you love to do.

Numbing Pain With Food

Many people who struggle with eating issues or weight problems find themselves eating at times when they are not really physically hungry. They may not even know why they are really eating.

This is painfully familiar to many people. Someone who is unable to stop a visit to the refrigerator, who finds a half-eaten bag of chips in hand, or who eats to the point of discomfort, may be trying to cover up or handle other problems with food.

Full And Quiet

It actually works for awhile. When eating, the physiology changes. Blood rushes to help digest the food as the stomach becomes full. This can temporarily stop a mind agitated with thoughts or a stomach jittery with anxiety.

This feeling of fullness reminds a person (on a subtle psychological level) of being taken care of as a youngster. It feels good to feel full—not empty or yearning.

It also feels good to be comforted. The person who eats is trying to make the bad feelings go away, to comfort herself. She feels like she is doing something—even if feeding herself might not be the most appropriate way of handling her feelings. Not doing anything makes her feel helpless or panicky.

Nothing Wrong Here

She is trying to stuff her feelings inside. Chances are, she grew up in a family in which feelings weren't talked about. She was probably reinforced for being pleasant and sunny, and shunned for expressing anything negative like anger or fear.

The problem with this is that she didn't know what to do when she felt anger and fear. These are real feelings that come up for everyone. But young girls are told they are not attractive and won't be liked if they are too negative.

When she felt fear or anger, what could she do? She had to keep quiet. Yet the feelings were still there. She had to make them go away somehow. So she turned to food. Her mother had comforted her with food before, so she tried eating. It seemed to work. At least it was better than nothing.

Sometimes, there were bigger, more frightening problems in the family that no one was talking about. Mom and dad's marriage was in trouble. Someone was being physically or sexually abused. Money was short. Still, no one talked about what was going on, and a picture-perfect image was put up for the world to see.

> *A person is set up to develop an addiction if she has only one way to deal with the stresses in her life. Overuse of any single coping strategy becomes addictive.*

As a consequence, this young girl never developed any skills for handling stress. As she matured and went into high school, college, a job, and a marriage, she found herself facing bigger and bigger problems. She still had no way to handle them. So she ate. She kept trying to quell those inner fears and anxieties with food.

Cross-Addictions

She probably tried other ways of numbing her pain, too. She might have started drinking or using drugs along the way. She might have become sexually promiscuous or become a shopping card abuser. She might have thrown herself into her school and work, trying to achieve recognition.

Through it all, she kept trying to put up her own perfect front saying to the world that everything was alright when really, inside, it wasn't.

There are lots of ways to unwind or escape the stresses a person is dealing with. There's nothing wrong with any of them necessarily, unless they are used in an addictive way.

If the purpose is to numb the mind and avoid stress, then the coping behavior may become addictive. Ultimately, if the addictive behavior is done more and more often, it begins to destroy a person's life. An addiction to food is no different.

Developing Alternatives

A person is set up to develop an addiction if she has only one way to deal with the stresses in her life. Overuse of any single coping strategy becomes addictive.

Developing many ways to cope with problems is essential to preventing or healing addictive behaviors. Talking with friends, going for walks, keeping a journal, and so on are all methods that people can use to cope with stress.

If there are real problems that need to be dealt with, however, and if a person has never learned healthy coping skills or how to express and deal with fear or anger, then therapy might be a powerful step.

Therapy can help identify the things that are troubling a person and practical, realistic ways of dealing with them. It will teach her real coping skills so that she no longer has to numb her pain with food.

Exercise: *Buy a card file and some note cards. Think of all the things you can do to comfort yourself and to unwind from stress. Make a card for each idea. One card might say (in big letters in the center of the card) "play my favorite record or tape." Another might be "take a long, hot bubble bath." Keep building your file until you have 20 or 30 other choices besides eating to manage stress. When you are under stress, go to your file for ideas to help you deal with the situation without exclusively relying on food to get you through.*

The Rage Response

*B*inging is not a graceful act. It brings us down to the most primitive level of feeling and action we ever experience.

We find ourselves in the kitchen. Before we know it we are in front of the refrigerator. Then we are in it. We are roaming through the containers of food, hidden pleasures, and endless sensations.

We open every cupboard and paw through boxes of crackers and bags of potato chips. We keep going. We move quickly. Hidden, private, we are careful to do this fast. We tear off a bite and then another. We rip and stuff. Harder. Faster. Bigger. More. And more.

An Angry Edge

There is an edge to our actions, a violence almost. What is driving this passion, this destruction? We are angry.

We are more than angry! We are furious! We are so mad we could spit! We could scream! We could hit! We could kill! We could throw up!

Supposed To Be Good

But we are "good girls." We are not supposed to be mad, especially at our mothers, fathers, boyfriends, friends, husbands, or children. They love us. We love them. Love means we're never supposed to hate them. Well why are we so full of rage?

We are sitting on all of the anger, from all of the times over the years that we got angry about something. Chances are, it was legitimate anger. Someone was probably unkind, neglectful, or even abusive. So, we have a right to be angry.

But we don't know how. We don't know how to talk about what we feel. People go away when we do. People make us feel ashamed or weak. People turn things around and make us feel like it's really our problem. So we shut up.

Besides, the anger we saw in our families was pretty violent. We don't want to be that violent. We know how much it hurts people. It hurts us, and we're afraid that we would be just as hurtful if we let our feelings out. So we shut up.

But the rage builds up and gets hotter and hotter. We're mad at them, but we can't do

> *W*e find ourselves in the kitchen. Before we know it we are in front of the refrigerator. Then we are in it.

anything about it. So now we get mad at ourselves, because we can't get rid of this anger. We're feeling out of control, and we don't like it. We don't like ourselves much either because we can't control our anger.

And so we eat. Each bite and tear rips and rages at our feelings about ourselves and those who have hurt us. We go numb. We lose awareness of time and our surroundings. We are like machines, churning, churning...beating away at ourselves and our pride...acting out the rage we feel inside at everyone and everything, including ourselves.

The Right To Be Angry

We really are angry. We really do have tempers. We really do feel hurt, pain, and rage. We are not just sweet, pretty, and wonderful to be around.

Coming to terms with our anger is one of the hardest jobs we have in front of us. We have to swim upstream to feel it. We have no idea how to express it constructively. But we can learn.

The first step is recognizing how angry we are. The next step is to get some help processing these feelings and learning how to deal with them without being destructive to ourselves or others.

Stepping into our anger is the beginning of stepping into our power. By recognizing it, we can learn to use it or release it as called for by the situation. This gives us a choice. This lets us stop beating ourselves up.

Exercise: *The next time you find yourself chewing or tearing angrily or desperately at your food, go somewhere in private and ask yourself why you are angry. Be patient—you probably will hear denial or confusion at first. Keep asking.*

If you really start opening up to yourself, you will probably find yourself in tears. Usually underneath rage is deep, deep hurt. If you find a very big anger or hurt inside that is too frightening to handle by yourself, find a good counselor or therapist. Get the feelings moving so you can begin to get unstuck with food.

No More Dieting

The New Year usually means a new diet. This is the year the pounds are going to come off, and we think they are going to come off by controlling every morsel we put into our mouths. We begin with firm determination. We are not going to let ourselves get away with anything this time!

But our grim and punitive attitude never works. The diet never sticks. The pounds we lose never stay off. The body-image and self-esteem we desire always remain illusive. Our egos take another bruising.

A Radical Plan

There is no way out of this endless cycle of diet and weight gain unless we quit dieting altogether. Unfortunately, this sounds like the most radical and frightening possibility of all.

Isn't it better to keep trying than give up? How can we be sure that we won't simply balloon up in size and feel even more terrible about our bodies? How can we be so irresponsible, lazy, indulgent, and weak? How can we ever give up dieting?

The Dieting Myth

We have been fed all sorts of myths about dieting from doctors, advertisements, celebrities, neighbors, girlfriends, and even our mothers. We have absorbed them all. We share everyone else's phobia about fat, and we also share their lack of knowledge about how our bodies work.

Once upon a time, someone observed that eating a lot caused weight gain, so it seemed reasonable to assume that eating less would cause weight loss. It actually does for the first day or two—and then the survival mechanisms of the body begin to kick in.

The Survival Program

Our bodies begin to work tremendously hard to resist the effects of our lowered food intake. They are programmed to stay alive, not starve. When we eat less, our bodies interpret that as a problem: *oh, oh, there isn't enough food anymore, so I better slow down until some more food shows up*. Our metabolisms slow down. We need less fuel (calories) to burn to accomplish our normal activities.

When humans were hunters and gatherers and dependent on the abundance of animals or crops, this adaptive mechanism was a

> *But our grim and punitive attitude never works. The diet never sticks. The pounds we lose never stay off. The body-image and self-esteem we desire always remain illusive. Our ego takes another bruising.*

blessing. In times of plenty, however, the body still interprets a decrease in food as a threat to survival.

When people advise eating less as a way to control or lose weight, they usually are completely ignorant about this powerful mechanism of the body.

Harder To Lose

With a decreased metabolic rate, it becomes increasingly hard to lose weight. Body functions begin to change immediately when we diet in ways we often cannot perceive. The body fights harder and harder to stay alive. That is why menstrual periods can stop or why someone can begin to feel cold. Body temperature is reduced and the hormones to make babies are seen as nonessential when survival is threatened.

When we go off diets, our metabolisms are still low. We still require less calories than before the diets. This means when we start eating normally, we are going to gain weight faster than ever. Most people gain back everything they lost and even a couple of pounds extra. Weight gain could occur until the metabolism normalizes, which can take a few weeks.

Ups & Downs Of Dieting

If we begin dieting right away again because we cannot tolerate the weight gain, we repeat the cycle. The second time around is worse because we are starting with lower metabolisms to begin with. This means it will be harder to lose weight the second time, and we will put it on faster when we come off the diet. This up-and-down cycle of weight gain and loss called yo-yo dieting, has only been understood in the last few years.

No wonder diet centers and programs keep encouraging us to diet! Since most people gain the weight back, these programs are guaranteed ongoing customers. And since each time it is harder to lose weight, we will need their services even more. By encouraging us to diet, diet centers know they'll be busy for years to come!

An Act Of Courage

Our mood and self-esteem keep bouncing up and down with our weight. We are trapped in a no-win situation: unless we agree to get off the merry-go-round.

Giving up dieting takes great courage! For most of us, it is the only weight management strategy we have ever used. But every expert in the field, every recovering person who has been addicted to food, and every person who has broken free of compulsive, disordered, or excessive eating knows that dieting does not work.

A healthy relationship with food can only come from learning to handle emotions and past hurt with other techniques and resources than food and relearning new eating patterns.

New Eating Patterns

These new eating patterns inevitably involve regular meals with balanced foods to insure we get enough of the various nutrients we require. They are usually accompanied by regular aerobic exercise done in moderation.

This advice is as old and familiar as grade school nutrition for most of us. The thing is, it works. It only failed when we started repeat dieting which lowered our metabolisms. Food seemed to be the problem, so we started thinking certain foods should be taboo because they were fattening.

No More Taboos

Once again, most experts recommend something radical. They suggest eating what you are hungry for and when you are hungry. That means you can eat cookies and ice cream or whatever you want.

This may sound terrifying! These are the foods you have so diligently avoided because you know you would go crazy if you let yourself eat them.

At first, you probably will go overboard with the foods you have restricted from your mouth and cupboards. Eventually, when you know you can have them whenever you want, you will not crave these foods every minute of every day.

Your body will eventually begin to tell you it needs vegetables and protein and good, healthy breads. It will tell you how much and how often. And when you learn to listen and follow its requests, you will find your weight stabilizing and food will no longer be at the center of your existence.

Sound far-fetched? Of course it does! It contradicts everything you have been brought up to believe. But it is based on the truth of how emotions and physiology work. You can remove yourself from the dieting cycle forever and find that weight no longer dictates your well-being.

Exercise: *Keep track of the number of times you hear or see references to dieting in one day. Count every conversation you are in or overhear, commercial you see or hear, product you walk by in the grocery or drug store, talk-show topic, and so on. If you can, do it over the course of a week. You may be surprised to discover how much pressure there is for thinness coming at us from all sides every day.*

Getting Off Track

In a personal struggle with food, there are times in which we are more in control of our eating than at other times. This is a reflection of the level of stress in our lives and the degree to which emotional issues are surfacing.

Breaking Free

If we have made a concerted effort over time to heal these issues by working with therapists or doing other forms of personal transformation, we have probably seen some real progress in the way we relate to food.

We may feel that we are beginning to have choices about when we eat and how much we eat. We can identify when we are hungry for food and when we are hungry for emotional attention instead.

For a long time, everything seems fine, and then all of a sudden, we are binging again without control.

We can start eating and stop when we want to. We know when we are comforting ourselves with food, and we don't beat ourselves up anymore. We have compassion for the scared little girls inside each of us who need reassuring, and we are willing to comfort them in many ways.

We are committed to listening to our feelings and we recognize that a signal to eat may really be a signal that something is bothering us.

This is true progress. It is vastly different than living as a slave to our various appetites which all get acted out with food. We can be proud of how much we've changed and know that it takes daily effort. We have to stay conscious and aware of what is going on inside us in order to make it work.

Internal Signals

So what happens when this all comes apart? How come there are times when everything we have learned seems to come apart at the seams? For a long time, everything seems fine, and then all of a sudden, we are binging again without control.

We have to remember that our binging behavior is a signal that something emotional is going on. In some way, our lives have changed and we are uncomfortable. We are in over our heads.

We are doing everything we can to keep things together. We might be successful to the point that it looks like we are handling things quite well. However, our eating tells us that we are overwhelmed on the inside.

One Step Back

When we come to a transition point like this, it is easy to be confused about what is going on. It looks like we have regressed. In fact, it is easy to start giving ourselves a hard time for getting off track. But as we have learned again and again in the past, something important and probably painful is going on underneath where we can easily miss or ignore it.

Very rarely does life evolve in a straight smooth line. That is why people talk about taking two steps forward and one step back. Occasionally, we experience some kind of challenge in our lives which seems huge and impossible to handle. Over time, we grow in strength and perspective until we can handle it.

Quiet Before The Storm

After this surge of growth, things seem quiet for awhile. We feel content. Of course, something else inevitably comes along to challenge us once again, and we repeat the whole process. We grow stronger and take pride in the gains we keep making.

When we are in the quiet plateau after a big period of change, it is easy to be lulled into thinking we have done most of our work. We think that life will be simpler from now on.

However, it never works that way. A new problem or conflict always arises which causes us to grow. After a while, it seems as if life is designed this way to help us become stronger, better people.

Relying On The Familiar

Why do we turn to food during transitions? We use food because it was our very first coping mechanism. We go back to what is most deeply ingrained.

During periods of great stress, we turn to what is simplest and what takes the least energy. We are using every ounce of strength and creativity to handle the challenge before us, so there is nothing left over to handle our conscious use of food.

Our adult sides are handling the stress while our childlike sides are feeling the panic. It is the little girls in us that need comforting so badly that they reach for food. Little girls don't know when to stop. They only know they feel bad. They aren't worried about the consequences, they just need to do something to stop being so scared. Food quiets the panic for a short while.

Ebb And Flow

When the numbness wears off, our awareness kicks back in and we feel terrible about the consequences of what we have done. We worry about the weight, about being discovered, and about being unable to control these passionate needs. But for now, it is all we can do.

In time, we have enough energy to notice that our eating is related once again to the stress in our lives. We begin to pay attention to the feelings that are tumbling about inside and to find other ways to comfort ourselves.

This creative process takes a commitment of time and energy. This is why we sometimes seem to regress during a crisis which is demanding all of our resources.

Surprisingly, the feelings we discover underneath may be different than before. They may be deeper and more powerful each time. We may have to find new ways of comforting ourselves and be more patient as we try them out. But eventually, we will again get back on track.

As our life ebbs and flows, our eating will change. If we have learned to use food to comfort ourselves, chances are we will occasionally do so for the rest of our lives, at least in periods of great stress. After we go through a few of these cycles, we will know that when we get off track, we can get back on again. Our detours are only temporary.

Exercise: *Find some time to be by yourself and reflect back over the events in your life. In your personal notebook, make a list of significant transitions or big changes as far back as you can remember. Keep them in chronological order. Now, remember when you began binging, restricting, overeating, or dieting. From that point on, mark your weight history alongside your life events history. Do the ups and downs of your body and/or eating behavior coincide with the times of change in your life?*

When Food Is Just Not Good Enough

There is an unconsciousness to almost every binge. We binge to forget. To turn off. To quiet pain. To get away from it all. To stuff the gunk back inside.

We want to turn off our thoughts and feelings, and the repetitive act of reaching, chewing, and swallowing allows us to numb our pain for a short while. This momentary relief is why we repeat the ritual of binging. Painful problems always return, however.

Blanking Out

Disordered eating accelerates because people spend an increasing amount of energy and time trying to escape by binging, purging, or starving. Every bite is an attempt to make things right again. But it just doesn't work. Eating is just not good enough.

Allowing ourselves to question or think about why we are eating is an act of great strength and personal insight. Too often, people with pain are completely unaware that anything is wrong.

Food only has the power to shut us down when we are not paying attention to what it is doing. When we want to escape, we quit noticing things. We sit in front of the TV lifting spoonful after spoonful and chewing mouthful after mouthful without even noticing.

When we take a minute in the middle of eating to notice exactly what is happening, we suddenly find out that we are not feeling better after every bite. It simply is not working.

Unconscious Habit

If that is the case, then why do we continue? We keep eating out of habit. We have learned to reach for food when we are upset.

We can also learn stop in the middle of an emotional eating episode to ask ourselves what we really need instead of this mechanical and mindless feeding.

Creating A Crack

By stopping for a moment, we create a crack. The smooth, uninterrupted act of binging is broken with awareness. With every crack, there is an opportunity for light. We can choose to become more enlightened by widening the crack and finding out what is really going on and what we need.

This takes courage because a crack signifies an opening into something unknown. We are very familiar with eating. Even if we don't like it, we feel safe because we always know what is coming.

Creating a crack is more significant than we might think. Allowing ourselves to question or think about why we are eating is an act of great strength and personal insight. Too often, people with pain are completely unaware that anything is wrong. They do not have the choice to stop and notice.

Questioning our thoughts and feelings means we are questioning the ways we learned to handle stress. Most of us have been taught to keep problems hidden because our families did the same thing. Very few people ever learn healthy, constructive ways of dealing with pain.

We have a choice about whether we are going to numb ourselves as we have been taught or whether we are going to embark on inner adventures to become awake and whole individuals.

The willingness to question is an act of sheer human bravery. It helps give us the first experience of power—that of discovering what is important in our lives.

Exercise: *The next time you reach for something to eat because you need comforting, notice something. Take a bite. Take a few bites. Eat however much you eat to numb yourself. But this time, somewhere along the line, stop for a minute.*

When you take a bite, you are supposed to feel better. Does it work? Take another bite. How good is it? Take another bite. Is it really working? By now, there should really be some positive effect besides a full belly. Is anything really happening? What can you try instead? What do you need now?

Eating Away From Home

Eating away from home can be one of the biggest challenges to face in the early phases of changing eating patterns.

When you are out for a social occasion such as a date, party, family gathering, office dinner, etc, it is harder to control all of the factors that affect your eating.

A Loss Of Control

The stress level is higher which makes emotions more intense. Old feelings from other uncomfortable situations may be triggered. You may be concerned with

> *Eating away from home requires planning ahead and a healthy dose of personal tolerance. There simply is no way that you have anywhere near the control over your choices about eating.*

making good impressions rather than with figuring out what you are really hungry for.

The choice of food may also not be good for you. There may be an array of your common binge foods. The food may not be very nutritious, so you can be hungry no matter what you eat. The gathering may have been scheduled early or late so that you had to eat twice or wait until you felt starved.

The atmosphere at gatherings is often not conducive for healthy eating either. There is too much noise and distraction to notice your needs. You may have to eat standing up, walk through long lines, order unknown dishes, eat to please a relative, and so on.

If you are not able to eat in a way that is healthy for you, then eating out can feel like a major setback in the progress you have

made. This experience is common, for example, on vacations, dates, visits home, or at business meals.

Since you may be away for more than one meal, eating while traveling is even more of a challenge than one event.

College or other group living situations can also present some of these same problems if people have different eating needs or if you have to eat someone else's cooking all of the time.

Be Prepared

Eating away from home requires planning ahead and a healthy dose of personal tolerance. There simply is no way that you have anywhere near the control over your choices about eating. It is much more likely that you are going to eat more than you want, at times when you don't want to, and feel unhappy about it.

Someone Else's Rules

The first key to handling this is to recognize that you simply cannot control things the same way you do at home. This may make you angry. It is important to acknowledge your frustration rather than to eat.

Once you have acknowledged how frustrating the circumstances are, it is also important to accept that you may find yourself eating differently than if you could make healthier choices.

You may go back to old habits, or simply make decisions about what to eat or how much to eat that do not fit what you want or what your body needs. It is important to be tolerant. This is not the end of your life. You can only do your best.

My Body First

When you find yourself eating away from home, try to approximate the way you would if you were at home. Try to eat at roughly the same times and try to choose the same kinds of food.

If you are at a restaurant or on the road, it is easier than you might think to request foods. Start by figuring out what would be best for you. Then try to find a place to eat that will let you make the choices you want.

If you are eating someone else's food that you cannot change, as much as possible, eat only the items and quantity you want. You do not have to eat to please.

Regain Your Power

After the event is over, think about what you could do the next time. Could you suggest another place? Could you arrive after the eating is over? Could you help plan a healthier selection?

Could you check out the menu ahead of time and find out if the chef can accommodate your special request? Could you socialize in a different way that does not revolve so much around food?

By reviewing what made you uncomfortable, you may discover strategies that you can use next time. This will make you feel more in control.

Unfortunately, it is probably impossible to always be in healthy eating circumstances. Too many people misuse food and are unaware of their feelings.

The best you can do is to be aware of what is good for you and make these choices whenever possible. If circumstances are not in your favor, you have to make the most of the situation until you can once again make your own choices.

Exercise: *Before you go out, take the time to imagine how the food will be at this event. When will you eat? What will be served? How hungry will you be? Will there be foods that will trigger you to overeat? Will there be healthy foods that will satisfy you? Will there be foods that you want to treat yourself to? How much do you want to eat? How much and what do you need to eat?*

Now, being as realistic as possible, decide how you can handle the event in the most positive way for you. Should you eat something before you go? Should you arrive late? Can you offer to bring some food so you know there will be at least one healthy choice for you? Be assertive as you imagine possible solutions. Chances are, there are a few things you can do to get through the occasion in a fairly positive way.

Getting High On Getting Thin

A person with an eating problem feels out of control in a world beyond her control. Everyone wants something different from her. She never seems to measure up to the expectations of her parents, friends, boyfriends, teachers, classmates, bosses, co-workers, or family members. She could always do something better. She thinks that if she was more perfect, people would love and accept her more. She would feel happier inside.

Empty And Unlovable

Instead, she feels empty, lonely, and unlovable. She reaches for the old familiar comfort of ice cream, pasta, chips, or chocolate. Before she knows it, things are out of hand. She is binging nonstop.

When it is over, she feels ashamed of her inability to control her lust for food. Her

> *She thinks that if she was more perfect, people would love and accept her more. She would feel happier inside.*

desire blinds her. She gets lost in the frenzy of eating. Although she actually wanted and needed to binge, afterwards she feels dirty and low.

For some, this secret affair goes on for years. Others take a different route, vowing to conquer the demon that rules their lives.

It begins with resistance. An impulse comes to eat, and the person doesn't give in. It might take every grain of strength she has to stay out of the kitchen or away from the vending machine, but somehow she does it. She buries herself in work. She grabs a cigarette. She pedals furiously on her cycle. She does anything to get away from the overpowering urge to eat.

Lo and behold, she does it! She gets through the moment, the afternoon, and maybe the whole day. The next morning, she wakes up ravenous, but her success yesterday spurs her on.

The second day is harder. Her thoughts spin with images of food. Her stomach churns. She gets a headache that gets worse as the day goes on. She is worthless at school and work. All she can think about is food.

Still she resists. She gets up a million times but always detours to the water fountain or library in the nick of time. Her battle is enormously difficult, but slowly the hours crawl by.

Strength To Resist

The evening is the worst. Her hunger is bigger now. She is not sure she can hang on, but she desperately wants this new life without eating. Her thoughts still race with food, but at least it is not going in her mouth. She exercises and cleans. She exercises some more. Finally, she tumbles into bed feeling shaky and slightly ill, but not full. She made it through day two.

The rest of the week is more of the same. She picks at a few lettuce leaves and rice cakes, drinks gallons of iced tea and diet soda, and allows herself a few grapes or an apple. She manages to get by so no one notices much.

She has seen the light. The scale is beginning to creep down to smaller numbers. Her clothes are looser. Most of all, she is feeling in control of her body. She has finally found a way to beat her hunger.

She feels good—in control, strong, full of power, capable, and proud of her achievement. Physically, it's another story. She is lethargic and moody, but she pushes on.

Instead of trying to please everyone else, she is pleasing herself. She is going to be the thinnest person she knows. Then everyone will envy her body and her willpower.

She gets used to her headaches, moodiness, and fatigue. She brushes it off as PMS or stress. She still finds her thoughts wandering to food, and she spends a large part of the day planning how to distract herself.

The routine is becoming more familiar. Sometimes, she even feels great. She never eats more than 600 calories a day and usually much less. Her endorphins are kicking in to help her survive. She skipped her period, but she didn't miss the mess.

Power Of Feedback

The comments from her friends urge her on. People notice her more than ever before. They can't believe how thin she is, and this makes her feel absolutely high. Finally, she found her place in the world. She learned how to crush her crazy eating.

There was only one problem. When she was alone, she had to keep moving or else she would eat or feel how alone she still felt. Her new success was not enough. She still wasn't happy, but she didn't know why. All she knew was that getting thinner made her feel the best she had ever felt, so there was no way she was going to stop.

Sometime later, she found herself in the hospital. Her body gave out. The body she had fought so hard to control was out of control again. People wanted her to eat. She couldn't. They didn't understand how

important it was to her to resist. Nothing had ever made her feel so strong, so worthwhile. Even if it killed her, at least she would die with her willpower intact.

Doubting Control

One day, someone told her that she really wasn't in control of food, her body, or her eating. Food was still running her life even if she wasn't swallowing it. This accusation enraged her, but she could not get the thought out of her mind. A bit of doubt about her life and choices began to creep in.

She pondered a long time while her body remained weak. She was at a junction point where she could choose to change. If she chose to keep resisting food, she would teeter between life and death, possibly for years. If she acknowledged that something important was still missing, she would have to begin a search that could mean confronting painful feelings.

She found that person who told her she was still at the mercy of food and began therapy. Her progress was slow. It was very hard giving up the one thing she believed she excelled at. She kept at it, and one day realized that her willpower was keeping her going in this new direction. She had not lost her strength! She was just re-directing it in a way that was much harder to measure.

This made her work even harder to change. She found herself trying new things and meeting new people. She knew she would make it: she was a fighter and a survivor.

In My Mother's Kitchen

*H*ave you ever noticed when you return to your mother's house, that you somehow become younger? Just walking through the door brings you back to feelings and behaviors that were part of your childhood.

Even though you have been out on your own making decisions, returning home means somehow becoming a little child again. You return to the role you played for all those years with the person who brought you into this life and raised you.

Early Patterning

That early relationship is so fundamental to who you are today. Patterns were imbedded day after day, year after year.

> *F*ood demonstrated our mothers' intense desire to nurture us. Their food was their love. To feel it, we had to eat it. To this day, we still eat to feel love.

It is no wonder that returning home to your mother's house is like entering a time capsule. You are brought back to replay out old roles and relationships.

This is particularly evident around issues of food. Many women who have struggled with food find themselves less in control in their mothers' homes than anywhere else. In fact, all of the gains they worked so hard to make seem to crumble in their mothers' kitchens.

A Flood Of Feelings

Mother doesn't even have to be there. Simply standing in the kitchen brings back a flood of unconscious feeling: of being fed and of not being nourished. These feelings may surface into images and words—or they may translate into impulses to open the cupboards and taste everything.

Tasting brings us deeper into memories. The familiar flavors and foods remind us of who we were, and we once again become our mothers' little girls. We are open and vulnerable. We take in their food, and we take in their way of loving us.

Mother And Love

Our mothers helped make us who we are: by shaping, feeding, and being with us. We ingested their strengths as well as their weaknesses. We learned to care the same way they cared—everyone else came first and people they cared for never went hungry.

Food demonstrated our mothers' intense desire to nurture us. Their food was their love. To feel it, we had to eat it. To this day, we still eat to feel love.

Best Intentions Wither

When we return home and resume old patterns of eating, we feel like we have lost control. We have worked hard to create a different relationship to food, but now all willpower evaporates. New patterns vanish. Best intentions wither.

Their cookies win us over. Their creamed soups warm our bellies. Their suggestions for second helpings seem completely sound, and we eat every morsel. Our eating pleases them. We are taking in their love. They know we know that they care. It is so primary.

Vulnerable Mothers

Our mothers are as vulnerable as we are. They need to feel our love as much as we need theirs. They don't know how to ask for it any more than we do. They don't know how to tell us their feelings either. We think they know, but they don't.

They are part of the same legacy of female silence we belong to. We have learned from them how to fit in. We know only what they know unless we have deliberately tried to develop new skills in therapy and other relationships.

Legacy of Silence

It is harder for our mothers to change than for us. They have been doing things their way much longer than we have been doing ours. We most likely will have to take the first step. This seems too hard. We have always relied on our mothers to make us feel safe.

Taking the first step toward building an adult relationship with our mothers means taking a risk. Our mothers may not respond to our first clumsy and self-conscious steps—either because they can't or they won't. They may be too afraid of changing the familiar order of things after all these years. They may not trust or believe in themselves enough to try. They may not even be aware that we want and need something different.

Creating Friendship

What we want is a new relationship. We want to know our mothers as women now that we are grown up. We want to talk and share feelings. We want to feel respected by our mothers for our accomplishments and our growth. We want to discuss our worries and hopes without receiving motherly judgement or direction. We want to hear about our mothers' dreams and disappointments.

Forging a new relationship isn't easy. Being a mother is full of great purpose and responsibility. Many women do not want to readily give up that sense of importance.

For us, being taken care of by our mothers can be the sweetest sensation on earth. It gives us a feeling of security and well-being. Many daughters do not want to give that up and lose the sense of adoration they receive from their mothers.

The old mother and daughter roles must step slightly aside and make room for new patterns, and we have to take the lead. We have grown up in a time when it was more permissible to explore and talk about feelings. We have had more practice.

A New Bond

What these new patterns will be like is unknown. However, honest, emotional communication always brings two women closer, even if they are mother and daughter. A bond of friendship can slowly be created on terms that are more equal than ever before.

When you return home again, you will still feel the child in you, but you will retain some of your adult power. There is now a place for your adult in the house. You are greeted by your mother, a woman and friend, rather than just your mother.

As an adult in your mother's house, you are free to eat as an adult. You may still choose to taste those foods that you remember so fondly from growing up, but they will not crush your current resolve. They will not erase your new patterns and power to make different choices for yourself.

Out Of Sorts With Food

*H*ave you ever noticed a time when your life felt all out of sorts? Nothing feels right. Something is off kilter, but you don't know what it is.

This is a subtle feeling. Since nothing particular is bugging you, it is hard to know what the real problem is. But you know there is one because you are eating, binging, and gaining weight.

For those of us who use food for comfort in emotional circumstances, feeling out of sorts is one of those uncomfortable situations that we don't know how to handle.

Uncomfortable Again

As we learn to recognize the relationship between feelings and food, we discover that we eat instead of expressing our anger to someone or dealing with the fear that we feel. We also eat to handle our loneliness.

*W*hen our lives feel out of kilter, it often means that an important need of ours is not being met. It may be a need we did not even realize was there. Our search helps us figure out what is going on inside us.

Anger, fear, loneliness, and sadness—these are feelings that can be identified with practice. When we find ourselves eating, we can ask what is really going on—what do we really need instead of another bowl of ice cream?

When we ask this question and we get no clear answers back, the process of healthy eating is harder. We have to double-check to see whether something is making us angry, hurt, afraid, or resentful.

If we still can't figure out what is bothering us, we have to dig deeper. Since the clues are always inside, we must identify the parts of us that are uncomfortable and find out why.

People gain personal insight in different ways. Some need to move their bodies (run, dance, or push furniture around) to untangle their thoughts and feelings. Others need to talk out loud. Many write thoughtfully. Some go right to their therapist to help them solve the puzzle. Whatever the method, the process will always lead to personal discovery.

When our lives feel off center, it often means that important needs of ours are not being met. It may be needs we did not even realize were there. Our search helps us figure out what is going on inside us.

Continuing Change

Over time, our needs change. Our life choices must reflect these changes or we will feel off balance again. We may think we have regressed because the old feeling of everything not being right is back again. We haven't regressed at all. In fact, it's just the opposite: we grew so much that our new choices are no longer adequate. We must learn to make another set of choices to fit our stronger selves.

Adjusting our lives is not new. Perhaps the first change we ever made was to commit to therapy once a week. Then we may have started a food journal. Next, we may have found a support group to attend. And on. And on. Step by step, change by change.

After much time and many changes, we get our lives into a healthier place. We settle into this new lifestyle with pride and confidence. It becomes normal. Eventually, we take our changes for granted. We assume this new combination is the right one for us.

It will be right for awhile, but as we change, we outgrow this pattern and need different lifestyle choices to fit new values and behaviors.

Emotional Quality

This may come as a surprise. We did not realize that we would keep on growing every day. We thought we fixed our problems, and we were grateful to finally feel comfortable with our lives. But when we find ourselves eating again, we know it is a signal for more change.

This time, the change may be more subtle. We may need more time for ourselves. We may need quiet to get in touch with inner feelings. We may need to play and be spontaneous. We may need to talk to friends, family, or our partners.

This new layer of needs is not directly connected to food, but it affects the quality of our emotional lives. So just like before, if we don't listen, our insides start churning. More and more often we feel hungry. And until we recognize the hidden message, we will eat.

As we grow, this pattern will repeat itself. We will have periods when we feel as if everything is finally in a healthy place. Before we know it, our bodies will send us clues that we need something new. Because these periods allow us to discover and express new dimensions of ourselves, they need to be recognized, welcomed, and worked with as soon as possible.

Exercise: *When you find yourself eating for no clear reason, set aside some time to have a heart-to-heart with yourself. Go for a walk, lock yourself in your room, climb into the bathtub, turn off your phone—make sure there will be no interruptions. Then, start talking.*

Ask the uncomfortable part of yourself what is missing or what is out of balance. This is just like talking to a friend. You may need to prompt yourself—is it this? Is it that? Are you feeling this? What do you need? How can we do it? But what if such and such gets in the way? How will we handle it? What are our options? And so on.

You will come up with some new ideas. You may find out exactly the new change you need. You may come up with suggestions to try for awhile. Chances are, you'll have to take time again with yourself later to continue the conversation and check in to see if the new changes are meeting your new needs.

Night Feeding

We have tried hard all day to stick to our resolve. To be good. To follow our plan. We ate breakfast. We ate lunch. We even had a snack late afternoon to handle our ebbing energy. We came home, read the mail, changed clothes, got something to eat, listened to the evening news...and then it happened.

Somehow, our plan got lost. Or maybe we didn't really have a plan. Anyway, the evening hours peeled away in front of the television. Mindless, heartless, empty time. We were tired and drained from the day.

Lumps on The Couch

We work hard to do our jobs right, make good impressions, keep up with schedules, get everything done, and keep everyone happy. It takes a lot of energy. Now, here we are. Lumps on the couch. Tired, depressed, and needy.

We want something sweet. We get some cookies. We want something salty. We make popcorn. We are thirsty. We pour ourselves

> *Why can we be so controlled during the day, and end up so undone that same evening? Our eating gives us the answer. We need replenishing and nourishing. We need to feed our emotion.*

some soda. We want something to eat with the soda. We grab some crackers. The cookies weren't sweet enough, so we make brownies. We have milk with our brownies, but now we feel so heavy. We want to feel lighter and clean. We pull out the oranges. And on and on. Our evenings spiral into oblivion.

A Trail Of Food

What happened? Why can we be so controlled during the day, and end up so undone in the evenings? Our eating gives us the answer. We

need replenishing and nourishing. We need to feed our emotions. It's as simple as that.

We give and give all day. We deal with stressful circumstances. We rise to every occasion. We handle whatever comes our way. At the end of the day, our energy is spent. Our reserves have been used up. The tanks are empty.

Unknown Signals

The only way we know how to fill ourselves is to eat. We do not know how to interpret the signals of fatigue and emptiness our bodies are sending to us in any other way. We do not understand that they are saying our bodies need refreshing. They need reenergizing. They need compassion.

We sense the fatigue and feed it with food to give ourselves energy. We sense the emptiness and feed it with food to fill ourselves up. But the fatigue was really emotional fatigue and the emptiness was really emotional, too, so feeding ourselves food is ineffective. We are still hungry. We try eating some more. We are still hungry. We try eating even more. It is all we know.

Reclaim The Night

For some women, this pattern goes on for years and years. It stops only when we reclaim evenings for ourselves.

When we go home at night or stop our chores, we are still growing, learning, and feeling beings. The evening is part of our waking time in which we can explore our potential, express who we are, and discover new talents we have. It is also a time to nurture ourselves, take care of wounds—both fresh and old and connect with resources and activities to replenish ourselves.

Night Needs

Too often, we think of evenings only as the end of the day. They are down time. Time to rest and relax before tomorrow's work begins again. If we unwind by shutting down in front of the television, all of the reactions to the day and the problems we are facing in our lives begin to fester.

These feelings need to be heard. Since they are not appropriate to come out at most work, school, or social settings, we need to create other time to deal with these very real and legitimate reactions.

Each of us also needs to express our creativity in many ways. Even if we are lucky enough to make our living doing something we love, most of us get bored unless we have variety. Our minds need to be stimulated. Our hearts need to be expanded. Our bodies need to move.

Chances are, our daytime activities do not meet all of these needs. In fact, they might make some needs greater. For example, if we sit all day, our bodies may need physical activity at night.

Our food plan fails in the evening because we need to feed ourselves in other ways. We need to comfort ourselves after a hard day. We need to nurture and replenish the energy we have given out. We also need to create opportunities to stimulate our capacity for growing.

More Than Work

We are more than our work. Whether we are students, housewives, employees, bosses, mothers, or even therapists, we have an incredible capacity for curiosity. We love to learn. We love to be interested. We love to be stimulated. And we want most of all to be clean—free of our painful, hurt feelings and wounds of the past.

These needs have to be heard and responded to in a respectful, loving fashion. Learning to listen to our whole selves and make plans to meet all of our needs must be part of our food plans.

A New Kind Of Plan

Does this sound crazy? Planning hot baths to comfort ourselves after a long day is part of a food plan? Yes! Planning to read a novel to let our hearts laugh and cry is part of a food plan? Yes! Planning to spend five minutes stretching, 20 minutes on an exercise bicycle while listening to a favorite album, and five minutes unwinding to a guided imagery tape that respectfully fills the body's need for activity and attention—this is part of a food plan? Yes! Planning to take a class, sew an outfit, or repot plants to do something different and interesting...this too is part of a food plan? Yes!

Creative Evenings

A food plan is not just about food. It is about a new way of living. Since our days are structured for us by other responsibilities such as school, work, household chores, etc., it is often easier to eat according to our plans during the day.

Our evening lives are just as important, however. As we choose to live and eat differently, we have to find balanced and satisfying ways to spend our evening time. If we are meeting our needs for creativity, comfort, variety, movement, healing, and learning, then food will not have to perform so many other roles.

Exercise: *If you find yourself overeating in the evening, turn off the TV, put down the donut, and ask yourself what is missing. What do you really need? What are you really feeling? Are you bored? Sad? Angry? Scared? Exhausted? Lonely? Overwhelmed?*

Is there something you could do right now to help change that feeling? Call a friend? Go for a walk around the block? Write in your journal? Put on a loud album and dance? Put on soft music, lie on the floor with your eyes closed, and flow into the music? Write a nasty letter to your boss and then burn it? Crawl into bed with the latest novel and go to sleep early?

Each evening is yours. It is precious time. Make it meaningful to you.

The Big Bottom Blues

All across America at this very moment, countless women are deciding not to go to the beach or pool because their bodies don't measure up. They cannot fit into the string bikinis, thong swimming suits, or lycra outfits they see on other women (who no doubt starve themselves or develop eating disorders). Their shame keeps them clothed, hot, and at home.

Standing in front of a mirror without clothes, we take a close look at the mounds our bellies make, the ripples in our thighs, and our well-rounded bottoms. Depression sinks in and we vow to change things. We try on all of our clothes to see if at least our bodies appear acceptable when we costume them appropriately—but nothing works. Outfit

> *Our hearts fill with pain knowing that we will never have the love we crave and desire because our bodies aren't fit to love.*

after outfit ends up on the floor. Finally, we collapse in tears of humiliation and rage. We are so ashamed of the shape of our bodies...and we hate ourselves for not being powerful enough to change them.

Tears Of Shame

Most of us forget that there are lots of body sizes. We see celebrities march across our screens looking beautifully anorexic. Their glamourous lives suggest that we, too, must look like them to get noticed. Thinly sculpted and seductively happy models cover the pages of the magazines we read while we eat lunch or relax before bed. To have success and romance in our lives, we come to understand that we must look like these women:

Men won't look at us unless we're thin. Companies won't hire us unless we're thin.

Bosses won't promote us unless we're thin. Friends won't hang out with us unless we're thin.

Our minds go wild imagining the emptiness of our lives without the right bodies. Our hearts fill with pain knowing that we will never have the love we crave and desire because our bodies aren't fit to love. Our spirits sink lower every day, every week, every month, and every year that we cannot coerce, coax, or court our bodies into a smaller size.

Our lives are tyrannized by this craziness. We focus on our bodies' seemingly uncooperative and obstinate natures and fear we will never have real happiness. We forget about the other hopes and dreams we have—a thin body must come first.

Restrained Desires

So we live on iced tea and salads all summer long. We long for pizza and malteds. We want to munch on pretzels, chips, and sno-cones, but we restrain our desires. We are proud of every small victory. Every day and every meal that we control our appetites gives us hope that one day, we will get down to the size we really want to be. We see that we really do have the power to change ourselves by changing our bodies.

We eagerly look forward to another day of restriction—only to find ourselves eating freshly baked cookies, ordering a hoagie or submarine sandwich, and eating an entire bag of popcorn. The stress is too much. Our willpower gives in, and our hope dies again.

On any given day, half the women in our country are dieting. Those who have lost weight are putting it back on. Most have clothes in their closets that are too small— waiting for the day they will fit again. Some women are throwing up. Others fill their bodies with chemicals hoping to change. A few haven't eaten for days to shed a few more pounds. More and more try surgery to change things once and for all. All the while, the makers of Ultra-SlimFast are getting very rich.

Something is wrong with this picture. We have been fed a vision of what women should look like that simply isn't right. A mandate that is impossible for the majority of women cannot be right. Expectations that make women ignore their natural hunger, fill with self-loathing, and spend countless hours and dollars trying to change, can in no way be supportive or healthy.

Yet we buy into it. We are seduced. Very few women have made true peace with the bodies they live in day to day. Most wish they could lose five, 10, 20 or more pounds. Most wish they looked different without clothes.

Why? We are used to pleasing, to trying to fulfill the desires of others. Through the ages, that has often meant adapting body shape or size. Beauty is different in each era and culture, but for eons, women have sought to please with their bodies.

Measuring Up

Today, when women's roles are undergoing rapid change, we don't always understand the new rules. We don't have the tools or perspectives to fit into the world in a way that brings us the personal satisfaction and happiness we seek. We feel overwhelmed by the choices and responsibilities we face and long for a simpler time.

Losing weight is simpler. Trying to become a size six seems more within our reach than finding work that makes us happy or a man that can accept and love us for who we are.

We are afraid that we won't measure up where it really counts, so we don't even try. We are afraid to express our talents, dreams, and wishes...because we are terrified of failure or rejection. We don't even take the first step. We accept that our world must be narrow, fixed, traditional, and without dreams. We fantasize instead about being loved because we are thin and pretty. We

focus on being attractive and keeping our bottoms small. When that doesn't work, our hope for happiness vanishes. We feel like we have sold our souls and we don't know why.

We have compromised our potential—the promises of our lives. The creative gifts that each of us have go unexplored and unexpressed. The world is waiting for women's creativity and nurturing, but we are busy bemoaning our fate in front of our mirrors. Trapped in bodies we cannot stand, we do not even see what is possible for our lives.

Across America, women are beginning to question the tyranny of thinness. They are giving up dieting. They are learning that they are beautiful whatever their size. They are refusing to bury their dreams in exchange for the promise of glamour, romance, and success. They want to be loved for who they are, not what they look like. They want to find a way to express their ideas, hopes, dreams, visions, and beliefs on their own terms. As each of us seeks more wholeness, we will find that our lives mean more when we are not focused on the size of our hips or thighs.

Exercise: *Every day for the next week or month, take some time to answer the following question(s):*

If I didn't spend so much time thinking or worrying about weight, food, or how my body looked I would

_____

If I was the size I wanted to be I would

_____

If I hadn't gotten sidetracked, what I would really like to be doing is

_____

If women didn't have to worry about how they looked the world would be different because _____

Fast Food Junkies

When was the last time you had real fresh steamed broccoli rather than rubbery microwaved or pale, dry broccoli from a salad bar? When did you make rice from scratch rather than use quick rice? Was your last taco homemade with fresh ingredients or from a frozen package?

On The Run

Statistics show that 45% of most people's food budgets are spent eating out. Much of that is food eaten on the run.

When we do anything on the run, the message is that it is not very important. We don't do an important paper or work project on the run. Hopefully, we don't see our friends only on

Important things take time. Eating is one of the places where we try to save time, but we end up shortchanging our physical and emotional health in the long run.

the run. We can't exercise or sleep on the run. Important things take time. Eating is one of the places where we try to save time, but we end up shortchanging our physical and emotional health in the long run.

The Cost Of Freedom

Fast food certainly has made life more convenient. Women no longer have to spend hours buying produce and fixing meals. This frees them up to attend to their many other career, school, personal, family, and social responsibilities. This freedom has allowed women to explore new aspects of their potential and lead richer lives.

Yet there is a cost. Packaged food is not nearly as vital as fresh food, so its ability to provide energy, nutrients, and healing elements is in question. We do not have any idea about the long-term health effects of the preservatives and radiation which is required to ship and store this food for us.

Food And Love

There is also an emotional cost. Food that is prepared and served with time and love is generally done in the company of other people. Eating proceeds in a more leisurely manner without a sense of rush to get on to the next activity. This assists digestion and full utilization of the food's nourishment to the body.

The taste of home-cooked food is also unmatchable (Sarah Lee would like you to think that her chocolate cake is as good as your grandmother's, but there is no match whatsoever.) The savory flavors of freshly prepared food, especially in the company of well-loved friends or family, gives us a satisfying sense of pleasure. We love a good meal for its ability to please us with smell, appearance, texture, taste, and comfort in the stomach. No wonder we are hungry!

McDonalds, Wendy's, Burger King, Denny's, and the multitude of similar establishments simply cannot fill the bill emotionally. They can give us the calories we need to keep going, but they cannot nourish our desire to thoroughly enjoy what we eat and feel nourished on all levels.

So we are left feeling hungry. We find ourselves late at night seeking the pleasure we know is possible with food by eating various delectables until we are satisfied or give up.

What often works is something that tastes homemade. Fresh pasta. A sinfully rich cake. Ben & Jerry's ice cream. Last night's home-cooked leftovers. No wonder eating disorders, weight problems, and compulsive eating are on the rise!

A Simple Test

Try gathering some friends or family together and do a pot-luck dinner or make a meal for them. Set the table, put fresh flowers on the table, turn on some lovely music. Socialize a bit before sitting down to eat. Enjoy each other's company all the way through dinner. Serve a scrumptious dessert and tea to top it off.

Now imagine you did the same thing but with take-out from Burger King or Wendy's. It just isn't the same. Even if you serve take out from a fancy deli, it still isn't the same as if you made it yourself.

Love makes food taste better! It sounds crazy, but it's true. Your love for your friends is a silent ingredient when you cook for them. It nourishes and bonds people to each other. When you cook yourself dinner, your loving attention to yourself gets included. If you use fresh ingredients to get the earth's nourishment, too, then the meal will be truly remarkable.

> *Exercise:* *Try replacing one fast food meal a week with fresh food you made yourself. Pack a lunch: make a sandwich out of some wonderful bread you got at your favorite bakery and other fresh ingredients. Cook dinner one night a week. Preferably, invite someone over to cook and enjoy it with you. Make homemade foods each weekend that you can enjoy all week. See if you feel better and more satisfied after each real meal.*

Love Letter To My Body

I cannot know how hard it is to be responsible for me all day every day. You take me and carry me wherever I want to go. When I get up, you get up. When I want to keep pushing, even though you are tired, you keep going.

Whatever I do to you, you figure out how to make it work for me. If I don't feed you properly, you still give me energy. If I don't sleep enough, you wake up anyway. If I don't get you out in the fresh air, moving and flexing, you never refuse me.

Even if I take you into polluted cities, stuffy offices, and smoke-filled restaurants, you keep breathing. Even if I only have time for fast-food, sugary treats, and no fresh vegetables,

I do not always honor my need to eat. I edit my desire for food. I monitor and measure the growth of each curve as it pushes against my clothes. I look in the mirror and wonder who would truly celebrate the curves of this body with me?

you still give me new energy. Even if I race around under stressful deadlines and jammed schedules, you keep up with me. I have never experienced faithfulness so concrete.

I often take you for granted, and I apologize. When you finally react to my abuse by getting sick or collapsing with fatigue, I realize that you, too, need loving attention. You have needs that deserve recognition.

I become more sensitive to your voice each time you demonstrate that you are not indefatigable or infallible. I practice

honoring your requests for regular nourishment and rest. I sense your pleasure as I keep you clean, scented, and soft.

As your needs become more clear to me, I struggle with my deepest biases and callous judgements. I struggle to see you as beautiful in every way. I know you dislike my judgement of your various shapes. You cringe when I call a part of you fat. You feel my rejection deeply. You know my shame intimately. Years of diets and hateful thinking have gotten that message home. Your hurt silently filters through every pore.

My judgement mimics the abusive judgements I feel from the social programming around me. For years, I have accepted the standards unconsciously and judged you harshly because of them. As I struggle to get more conscious, I release their fierce grip with each new realization. Yet I am not free. I do not always honor my need to eat. I edit my desire for food. I monitor and measure the growth of each curve as it pushes against my clothes. I look in the mirror and wonder who would truly celebrate the curves of this body with me?

I am grateful that your strength keeps me going as I learn about myself. Your patience during every crazy phase has enabled me to grow, broadening my perspectives and strengthening my values. This slow and labored path is bringing me back to appreciate you.

I am thrilled to have you carry me through each day. I tuck you in lovingly with me each night and listen for what you need from me. Would it have been better for you if I had done something different (*how I ate, how I reacted to stress, how much I did, or when I stopped*)? Do you need something from me now?

Each loving act I do for you comes back to me. I can feel you relax as I oil my feet or dab flowered scent on my neck. You unwind and float to healing music and light. You revive when I lovingly serve you whole, healthy food.

You are my partner. I learn from you about myself. I learn about my pace. I learn about nurturing and neglect. I learn to recognize nonverbal cues and respond.

I pledge to keep practicing. I can only heal as you heal. So I vow to continue supporting you each day in a way that will allow my full energy, creativity, and hope to come alive. As you faithfully carry my mind, heart, and spirit, I embrace your will to live with quality.

Stress-Breakers

"*Over time, our needs change. Our life choices must reflect these changes or we will feel off balance again. We may think we have regressed because the old feeling of everything not being right is back again. We haven't regressed at all. In fact, it's just the opposite: we grew so much that our new choices are no longer adequate. We must learn to make another set of choices to fit our stronger selves.*"

Stress: Our Personal Underworld

Most of us have no idea how stressed we are. We get used to functioning with tension, nervousness, anxiety, and fear.

Stress is all around us—in the noise and traffic of city life, in the demands of a supervisor, and in the reactions of strangers as well as family and friends.

But stress really comes from our reactions to these pressures of daily living. Think about a day when you felt pretty good. The drive into work did not bother you at all. If someone was rude, it rolled off your back without any effect. Another day, the same drive and the same traffic can set your teeth on edge, particularly if you already were tense!

In other words, the stronger, more rested, and calmer we are, the easier it is to handle the responsibilities and incidents of our lives.

Healthy Stress Management

Stress management is critical to living a healthier and happier life. For people who use food to cope with stress, learning healthier ways to manage stress is crucial to changing eating patterns.

The key to stress management is restfulness of the body—which makes it stronger, and calmness of the mind—which makes it easier to figure out what to do.

Stress management begins with getting enough sleep, nutritious food, and exercise. All three of these basics have a positive and immediate effect on the strength of our bodies and the clarity of our minds.

If our lives are still too much to handle even if we lead a pretty healthy routine, then it is time to learn a relaxation technique for stress management.

Body-Mind Connection

Our minds and bodies have a very close relationship. You have probably noticed that if your mind is racing with worry about something, your heart beats faster and your breathing speeds up. You have probably also noticed the opposite: when the problem that was worrying you goes away, you can "breathe easier."

Relaxation techniques teach you how to calm both your mind and body so that you can handle things easier and with less lasting stress. You can find classes in most adult education or YWCA/YMCA programs. Many bookstores carry cassette tapes which teach you techniques to relax.

For people who use food to cope with stress, learning healthier ways to manage stress is crucial to changing eating patterns.

Taking time each day to practice relaxation when it is most convenient like before work, at the lunch hour, when you return home, or before bed, will begin to help you culture a new way of reacting to stress. You will find that your body has the power to change its reactions to stress, and so does the mind.

Changing Stressful Eating

Try a short period of relaxation just before eating. You will notice that some of your stress and tension can be relieved by relaxing. Rather than using food to try and numb these feelings, you are now beginning to give yourself an alternative way of handling them.

Sometimes during relaxation periods, you will find yourself going over a particular problem. The solution may come to you in the next few hours or days. If the problem feels bigger than you can handle right now, you may want to seek a professional to help you sort it all out. You do not have to do everything alone.

Once again, you are creating an alternative way of handling stress than with food. This is the beginning of changing your eating pattern.

Exercise: *Lay down and close your eyes. Begin from the top of your head and relax every muscle of every part of your body. Work your way slowly to your toes. Keep your eyes closed. Let your breathing slow itself naturally. Breathe deeply in and out. When you have relaxed all the muscles in your body, remain with your eyes closed for another five minutes just breathing easily. When you are ready, get up slowly.*

This process can take anywhere from 10-20 minutes. If you like, put on some gentle, soothing instrumental music while you are practicing this relaxation.

Editor's Note: My personal favorite is TM (Transcendental Meditation). It is easy, takes 20 minutes twice a day, and the impressive results are noticeable immediately.

Exercise For Energy

*A*dding exercise to a daily routine has more benefits to our psychological and physical well-being than one could ever guess. Although there is a big fitness craze going on, many people have still not found exercise routines that work for them.

Others have taken it too far. An addiction to exercise is important to recognize as an means of escaping from life's pressures as well as to burn off calories.

A Personal Tale

My first experience with exercise was organized gym. It started in grade school and continued through my sophomore year in high school. I hated it. I had never been one of those running, jumping little kids, so I was not very familiar or comfortable with what my body could do. I was clumsy and awkward.

The teachers made me feel like the point of personal movement was winning—someone had to be best. At first, I was competing against grade school boys who were naturally athletic and later against female classmates who seemed as coordinated as the guys. I didn't stand a chance. I came out feeling like a loser with low body-esteem.

So physical education taught me not to like or trust my body. Because I felt so uncomfortable, I assumed I was just not good at sports. My friends helped me celebrate the last day of gym because I was finally free of that humiliation.

Finding My Body

I later went on to college only to find out I had to take three physical education classes to graduate. I groaned, put them off until the last three quarters and then took golf, modern dance, and swimming. I felt just as clutzsy in golf and modern dance, but

something different happened to me in swimming. I connected to my body for the first time in my life.

Having grown up on the lakes in Minnesota, I felt comfortable being in water and moving. When we started doing lap swimming, I could do it well even though I was not fast. Even more amazing, I found a rhythm and enjoyed myself.

Finding that rhythm was a critical breakthrough for me. I could keep going. I learned that my body could do something physical at its own pace. I started going to the pool voluntarily and swimming a few times a week.

Clearing The Mind

When I started exercising because I chose to, I had another breakthrough. As I settled into my easy lap rhythm, I found that my

> *F*ind something that you like, do it at a pace that is comfortable, start slow, and build up. Avoid pain. Listen to your body.

mind began to go over what was happening in my life. My swim time became my think and feel time.

Nothing interrupted me. No one demanded anything. I had quiet, personal time to work on problems or new ideas. I came out of the pool physically alive and exhilarated and mentally refreshed.

I continued to swim as long as I lived within a comfortable commuting distance to a pool. I swam before or after work, or even during lunch hour. Eventually, my life changed and it was no longer easy to get to a pool. I could not let go of that wonderful time to wake up my body and listen to my mind.

I decided to try running even though I hated girl's track with passion. But I could run wherever I lived or traveled, and it didn't cost anything except for the shoes. So I tried it.

Without Pain

The first day I got around one small city block, and then I had to quit. By now, I had learned that I would exercise regularly as long at it was at my own pace and without pain. After one block, my lungs and muscles were in pain. The next day, I tried going another block. I quickly built up to six blocks and then a mile.

One night, I had the same experience I had had while swimming—I found a rhythm and felt that I could go forever. It was very exhilarating! I was hooked. I became a daily runner going only one to three miles, and never very fast.

An Important Tool

While I run, I have the same private mental time I used to have while swimming. I treasure this time and find that if I don't run regularly, I am not able to handle the stresses of my life as well. It has become an important part of my wellness and stress management routine.

I try and run along a beautiful route so that I can have the added joy of natural surroundings. I run in every place I travel to (even Taipei in Taiwan), and I run in almost any weather. If the snow gets too deep to have safe foot placement, I switch to cross-country skiing. Once again, I can go at my own pace and do it almost anywhere there is snow.

These discoveries let me become comfortable in my body. I now enjoy other sports, too, at a pace that fits my needs and abilities.

Feeling Connected

Discovering my body and its abilities has made me feel more connected to it. It is easier now to hear when my body is tired, hungry, or hurting. Because it is an important part of me, I try to treat my body respectfully and give it what it needs. It in turn helps me to handle stress better and gives me clues as to what is bothering me. I can no longer imagine a routine without some physical activity.

Exercise: Even people who feel clumsy have the ability to discover their own athletic potential. It doesn't matter what activity a person tries. Walking is the cheapest and easiest to do anywhere at any time. It is also great exercise.

Find something that you like, do it at a pace that is comfortable, start slow, and build up. Avoid pain. Listen to your body. You will build strength and endurance with regularity rather than with pain. Then simply enjoy the feel of moving your body and the private time.

The Power of "NO"

Feeling stressed usually means being on overload. You know the feeling—jittery, on edge, panicky, angry—like you are going to snap inside if you have to handle one more thing.

Everything's going at maximum intensity. Your body is pumping. Every cell is awake and ready to fight or escape. Your heart and adrenal glands are working overtime. When you finally let your guard down, you will be exhausted.

This is no way to live. Yet most of the time, when we are under stress, the drama is going on in private inside our minds and bodies. No one else knows how bad it is.

When our bosses, kids, or friends want us to do just one more little thing, they have no idea that this might be the straw that breaks the camel's back. But somehow, we keep going, we get by.

We hate to say no. We don't want to disappoint anyone. We are afraid they may get angry at us. We are scared of rejection, and we are terrified of being abandoned. We've had too much neglect already in our lives.

Fear Of Rejection

So we say yes. It doesn't matter that we are doing more than anyone else. It doesn't matter that we are really doing someone else a favor. It doesn't matter that they are taking advantage of us. It doesn't matter that we shortchange our abilities to fulfill our own needs or responsibilities.

We say yes. We have been raised to be nice, to please. We have become very good at noticing how others are feeling and reacting. We are great listeners.

We liked the praise we got when we were younger for helping out at home, for not getting in the way, for being seen and not heard. It was the only form of attention we ever got.

Performance Love

People like us for helping out. They like to be able to count on us. When we do things for them, it makes them feel good. We like them to feel good. We like them to like what we are doing. It is the only kind of love we know.

This is performance love. We get noticed and accepted for doing things that please others: good grades, an orderly household, productive work, or a friendly smile. We can't risk saying "no" because it will take away the only love we know.

By never saying "no," we allow ourselves to be servants to others. We serve other people's needs without them giving equally in return.

> *We are scared of rejection, and we are terrified of being abandoned. We've had too much neglect already in our lives.*

This undermines our self-esteem. We know we are not being treated with the respect and dignity we crave. We know we are not appreciated for who we are as individuals, but rather for what we can do for someone else.

When we let people take advantage of us like this, they keep asking for favors. They may not even realize that they are putting us out in any way. We have to stop the cycle ourselves.

It makes no sense to get angry. We have to take responsibility for letting the situation be what it is. We also have to take responsibility for changing the situation.

How? By figuring out what is good for us. We have to notice when we are too tired or too overloaded. We have to listen to our inside reactions when we don't really want to do something. We have to *hear* our bodies, minds, and hearts.

Next, we have to dare say that we are too busy right now and can't fit their request in. We have to have the courage to say we would really prefer to do something else.

What can we expect to happen? First, we are going to startle the other person. They never heard us say "no" before.

They may try and talk us into doing something. We have to repeat what we said before and stand our ground. Gently, evenly, and in a normal voice, we repeat what we said.

These people may get mad at us. They may feel like we are being uncooperative or insensitive to their needs. We must gently and evenly respond that we need to do something else right now. We are sorry that they did not realize we were busy, but we are.

If they are really our friends and not just friendly with us because we do things for them, their anger will blow over. They were just taken by surprise.

If they are close to us, we can actually even tell them we are trying to manage our time

and workload so that we can live in a healthier, more sane way. If they care for us, they will understand and maybe even admire what we are trying to learn.

No is a very powerful word. It sets boundaries. It limits what people can take from us. It gives us a sense of strength and self-respect. We are treating ourselves with the dignity we deserve.

Exercise: For one week, keep a notebook that monitors how many times you say "yes" to other people's requests. Make sure you record even simple things like ordering something at a restaurant that someone else wanted to taste or split. Leave a blank column beside each event.

On top of the column, print the question, "Did I really want to do that?" Answer the question for each event. Now, for each event, write down what you could have said to express what you really wanted. Say them outloud. Imagine what the other person would have said in return. Imagine the worst thing they could have said. What could you have said in return that would not cause a fight? Now imagine them saying something that indicates everything is ok.

Try this out in real life with someone you trust.

The Ability To Self-Soothe

Everyone with eating or food issues is trying to cope with emotional pain. Feelings, past and present, churn beneath the surface and cause a person distress.

In order to diminish the pain, people turn to food. It is an act of comfort, largely motivated by family food rituals, old memories, and habits. We were comforted with food when we were young. Our family used food to express or cover over feelings. For years now, we have used food to handle stress.

We are looking for comfort, for something to make us feel better. We want our worries and fears to go away. We want to feel the soothing concern of someone who cares for us. We wish we could be held and have our hair stroked lovingly while someone assures us in a whisper: *It will be alright.*

A Lack Of Care

People with eating issues often did not receive the nurturing they needed as children. They were deprived of the simple, caring gestures and assurances that are central to caretaking.

They may be products of parents who did not know how to express their love because they were not nurtured either. They may have been born at a time of great conflict so they became lost in the shuffle—there was simply not enough left over to show love to another little one.

There are endless reasons why, but the result is the same: the child feels alone, unloved, unlovable, and unworthy of attention. That little child grows up into an adult that feels the same way.

Generations Of Pain

That little child also never had the opportunity to learn how to comfort or to soothe herself because there were no models to learn from. Children learn by copying what they see the adults doing around them. That is how behavior is passed down, generation to generation. A child who has not been soothed, does not know how to soothe herself or her children.

Being able to self-soothe is a critical skill for every adult. We are long past the stage when we can turn to someone to comfort every little hurt. Our friends and spouses can help in many situations, but not in all.

Comforting Ourselves

Expecting friends and family to provide all of our emotional comfort is a burden. That is like expecting them to "mommy" us. We remain childlike instead of maturing to take

> *Being able to self-soothe is a critical skill for every adult. We are long past the stage when we can turn to someone to comfort every little hurt.*

responsibility for ourselves.

Being able to comfort or soothe ourselves requires that we can do things to give ourselves the feelings of being comforted or soothed. We can calm ourselves. We can say loving, hopeful things to ourselves. We can create the feelings we had or should have had when we were little. What is comforting may be different for every person. But there are some universal elements.

A Little Attention

First, it is probably the little child in us that is hurting, so the adult side of us needs to hear that hurt rather than put it down. Our hurt needs to be acknowledged rather than denied.

Sometimes parents don't want to be bothered with their kids' needs. We do the same thing to ourselves. We don't listen to fears and concerns. We think we are too busy. We think it is stupid to feel bad about something.

We put down that little child side of us again and again. That is not soothing. The little child just wants to be heard. A little attention goes a long way. Taking the time to feel feelings, hear our worries, and notice what is bothering us is an important first step.

Bodily Comfort

Next, bodily comfort is key. Soothing a child usually involves a hug or being held. There is a feeling of warmth and being nourished. Children are sometimes actually even fed when they are upset. This is one reason why we learn to use food to comfort ourselves.

Instead, we can use bodily comfort to soothe ourselves. Getting into comfy clothes, taking a warm bath or shower, making tea or hot milk, cuddling up in a big chair with a good book, and so on, are all ways to provide comfort. Self-soothing may include recognizing that we need to have fun.

If so, go to a movie, go outside and ride your bike, stick your feet in a puddle, run through the sprinkler, fly a kite, make cookies, go to an amusement park—anything to make you feel more light-hearted and happy again.

Talking Out Feelings

At the risk of sounding silly, we might even talk to ourselves. Most of us need to talk out these concerns (*tell mommy what's wrong*). Just by saying them outloud, it helps to relieve the pressure and hurt that gets bottled up inside.

If we have close friends we can talk to, then calling them up is a great way to help ourselves get what we need. If there is no one around, we can actually have a conversation in our heads—or even outloud—between the side that is hurting and the adult side that is wise and comforting. You may feel funny doing this at first, but there is no harm. You are doing this to air out your feelings and comfort yourself.

Self-soothing may also mean you recognize that what you are dealing with is very big—too big to handle in these smaller, more homey ways. It may mean arranging to find a therapist or other professional who can help. Support groups can also be great sources of comfort and strength for individuals dealing with bigger, ongoing issues.

As we learn more about ourselves and get stronger, our ability to self-soothe grows. This means our compulsive coping behaviors can loosen their grip on our lives just a bit. Over time, we feel better taken care of by ourselves than ever before. We learn to trust and depend on our own ability to support and comfort ourselves.

Exercise: *As you read this article, is there a suggestion that you find appealing to do when you are hurting? Can you think of something that might work better for you? Identify it as one way to handle painful situations. Try doing it right now. See if you feel a little better, more nurtured.*

Make a commitment to do this same soothing activity the next time you are hurting from something. When the feeling becomes a little less intense, look back and see if your self-soothing activity helped. What you will probably find is that you need to do a combination of things. Experiment to find what works best for you.

A New Focus: Life, Not Food

Too much of our focus and energy is spent on worrying about our bodies and weight. At times, these issues seem to take most of our concentration and personal effort for improvement. Thoughts about food dominate our minds. We continually battle to resist these thoughts.

If we want to change this dominance of food in our lives, it is important to recognize that we are not one-dimensional. We are individuals that are much more than just bodies. If all of our focus goes to our appearance and weight control, then we are leaving other areas of our lives unattended.

Many Needs To Notice

We have creative talents which we use and develop in school or work settings. We have relationships to nurture at home and with friends. We need new ideas and experiences. We also need to feel a part of something larger, with greater meaning.

These other dimensions of our lives need focus and attention, too. They are often forgotten or overshadowed by our concern for weight-related problems.

If our concentration on food and weight has become an obsession, then the other areas of our lives are definitely suffering. It is simply impossible to be obsessed by body issues and still provide the attention that the rest of us deserves.

One strategy for diffusing the obsessive power that body and weight concerns have over us is to become committed to improving another dimension of our lives.

Loosening The Grip

If you are bored at work or in school, perhaps you are not really using your talents. If you feel stuck., decide to make a change even if it means taking less pay or getting a degree later. This may give you a personal boost of excitement because you are finally pursuing your dreams.

It does not matter which part of your life needs more attention. It could be relationships, health, career, spiritual development, living environment, hobbies, and so on.

If our concentration on food and weight has become an obsession, then the other areas of our lives are definitely suffering.

The key is to focus on something that really requires more attention. It is probably what is most dissatisfying about your life. Start there and begin to make a plan for improving that area.

You may even find that turning your attention to developing another aspect of your life may lessen your obsessive use of food because you are no longer as frustrated or unhappy. You are acknowledging your needs.

If this was part of the problem all along, your focus on food would have never solved the problem. You had to listen to the other parts of yourself in order to regain any balance.

Exercise: Sit quietly with a piece of paper and think about all of the aspects of your life: work, friends, family, health, fitness, eating habits, nutrition, creative interests/hobbies, education, and spirituality. In general, think about who you are, how you handle these aspects of your life, what you want to be different, the direction you are growing in, and what new behaviors, etc, you want to commit to. Now, pick a category to really focus on. Think about what would really make you happier and fulfill your needs. Identify a list of things you can do to begin filling these needs. Pick one to three things you can begin on right away. Make sure your goals are achievable!

111

Time For Myself

Taking time to meet our own needs is often very hard for women. We are trying to balance the multiple duties of being female: work or studies, love, friendship, family, personal fitness/beauty, and social activism. To keep everything going well requires a superhuman effort. Today's woman is very impressive.

But she suffers a lot, too. She often forgets to take time for herself because there isn't anything left over. Who has time to keep a journal or to take an evening bath?

Unfortunately, most women do not build private, personal time into their schedules. In times of zealous achievement, breaks have to be scheduled! We have to make conscious efforts to relax and unwind.

Here are some great suggestions to begin your process:

15-MINUTE Personal Breaks

Read A Book
Send Someone A Short Letter
Pull Weeds In Your Garden
Take A Bath
Play A Favorite Album
Relax From Head To Toe
Water The Plants
Pet Your Cat Or Dog
Write An Entry In Your Journal
Straighten Your Closet
Read A Magazine
Walk Around The Block
Call A Friend
Practice Tai Chi

The energy and refreshing outlook we gain from replenishing ourselves is well worth the investment. We will feel better and be able to give more to our work and relationships if we take time to put something back into ourselves.

Exercise: *Sound impossible? Try doing something to replenish yourself everyday for a week and see how you feel. Read a book for 15 minutes before you sleep. Walk around the block after dinner. It doesn't have to be big, but it should be enough to make you feel you have some time for yourself.*

We Try Harder

In our zeal to show ourselves and the world that we are capable, intelligent, and deserving individuals, we try harder. We put in extra time at work or school, we keep our friendships going and our bodies in shape, and we keep up on what's happening around us.

Super Achievers

We are overachievers. We make sure that we have done the best we absolutely can to win approval and avoid criticism.

We seek the approval of others because we never developed a sense of security as we were growing up. Things were too stressed in our families. We didn't hear often enough that we were loved. We did not form an internal sense of how delightful and adorable we are.

So we continue to seek acceptance and love by being approved for what we do instead.

Too Fragile Inside

We try so hard to create a positive response from others partly because we are deathly afraid of criticism. Our sense of self-worth can easily be fractured by a simple look or a few disapproving words. It doesn't take much to demolish any confidence we have worked hard to build.

Other people say we are too sensitive. We let little things bother us too much. We take everything too seriously. They are right. We are too sensitive, but we can't help it. They don't know how tiny and helpless we are inside because everything looks fine on the surface.

Success Means Impress

The only confidence we have comes from others saying we have done well. We learned to impress people with our ability to accomplish things. So we keep finding new things to do, and we make sure we excel.

Doing such an outstanding job all of the time is tiring. It has its rewards, but it takes away ordinary spontaneity, relaxation, humor, and joy.

As overachievers, we are generally not people who can sit on a couch and do nothing. We feel guilty reading the latest novel. We have to be doing something constructive, or we feel we are wasting time.

> *We try so hard to create a positive response from others partly because we are deathly afraid of criticism. Our sense of self-worth can easily be fractured by a simple look or a few disapproving words.*

Taking A Break

We know how to put all of our energy into making a good impression, but we don't know how to unwind. It is much harder than working! We have to learn to play and take breaks. We have to learn that relaxation is important, too.

We worked so hard to become adults. We wanted to enter the world of our parents so that finally we could win their approval. We worked hard to be serious and not silly. Now it is time to become kids again.

We can start slowly by walking barefoot through the grass or swinging on swings in the park. We have to dare to give ourselves permission to let our guard down and play.

Playing is really an attitude. It is finding the fun in little things. It means indulging ourselves just a little. It means not being so serious about everything. It means learning to laugh from our bellies.

With practice, we can welcome our childlike sides back into our lives. We will benefit immensely from this happy energy and openness. It will help make us whole people who experience joy along with our success.

Exercise: *Go to the video store and rent a movie for kids. (Suggestions: Neverending Story, Little Mermaid, Teenage Ninja Mutant Turtles, The Princess Bride, Black Beauty) Go home and sit yourself in front of the television in your most comfy clothes. Let your inner child watch the movie along with the adult side of you. Let yourself get completely into the movie—talk, cry, laugh, and get scared. Notice how good it feels to be so innocent with your reactions.*

You can bring this same kind of simple enjoyment to watching kids on the playground, reading a comic book, riding rides as the local fair, running through the waves at a beach, jumping into a pool, and making a big splash. Keep trying new ways to be childlike again.

Queen For A Day

There are very few times in our lives that we are individually honored. Unless we are mothers or fathers, the only days that are uniquely our own are birthdays.

We don't have to wait for birthdays and hope friends or family treat us the way we desire. Anytime we want, we can decide to designate one day as our very own special day and treat ourselves like royalty. This might seem too selfish or self-indulgent, but everyone deserves a special day.

Do What You Want

Think about it. What if you could spend a day doing only what you really wanted? What would you do? Going through the fantasy of creating your own day is very revealing. It might show you what gives you pleasure or what is missing from your daily routines. Go ahead—plan a day that would truly please you.

Perhaps you would sleep late and then have breakfast in bed. After a leisurely bubble bath, you would put on your favorite sweats and go for a walk in the park. Then it would be time to make lunch, set it out on a tray in the backyard with a tall glass of iced tea under a tree, and read a good, juicy novel.

That evening, you have a girlfriend come over, rent two videos and order take-out. Later, you make tea or cocoa to wind down before bed, put on your favorite album, and slip into your favorite nightgown. A perfect day.

Someone else's perfect day might begin by bounding out of bed early and taking a long bike ride into the country. She packs her lunch, swimming suit, and pens and paper to write a few letters to old friends.

After a wonderful day outside, she returns home and showers, rubs herself down with a scented body oil, and gets into comfortable clothes. She heats up her favorite dinner and enjoys it with a glass of white wine. She calls her best friend, talks for a few minutes, and ends her day by catching up on magazines that she has been wanting to read.

A third person might decide to get a massage in the morning and then meet a group of friends for lunch at a local restaurant. She spends an hour or two talking and then

Going through the fantasy of creating your own day is very revealing. It might show you what gives you pleasure or what is missing from your daily routines.

decides to stroll through a nearby shopping center to window-shop. That evening, she has asked her partner to make dinner for her at home and then take her dancing.

What makes each of us feel wonderful will obviously be very different. By letting our desires and imaginations create a perfect day, we have the power to make ourselves feel royal, honored, happy, and special.

Exercise: Set aside one special day to treat yourself like a queen. Plan how you want to spend it and then do it. After awhile, try it again. You may find a day like this is so reviving that it is worth doing once every season or even once a month. If you want to do it more often, you could pick a regular evening or afternoon.

A Change Of Scene

Many of us resist change because it takes too much energy, and it is frightening to begin something new. Sometimes, however, a change of scene does us a world of good.

As we commit to healing and becoming whole people, our feelings about ourselves get more and more positive. We learn to acknowledge our good points. We come to feel that we deserve happiness and love. We are more caring toward ourselves and our bodies as we learn to like ourselves more.

Committed To Healing

We express this care in many ways. We choose healthy foods that make us feel good.

We are more caring toward ourselves and our bodies as we learn to like ourselves more.

We take time out to relax. We talk to our friends to nourish our hearts. We play music and dance in the privacy of our bedrooms.

As we feel better about ourselves, we naturally want everything in our personal worlds to be healthier, too. We want to associate with people who acknowledge our positive qualities. We keep our kitchens and cars cleaner because we feel cleaner inside. We use more color when we get dressed because we feel better. We add plants and decorations to our rooms because we feel more attractive.

Choices For Health

Eventually, we want everything around us to feel healthy and supportive. We want to take classes that truly interest us. We want to quit working for abusive employers. We need to live with people that care about us. We want to see daylight and breathe clean air. We want a relationship that is respectful, accepting, and supportive.

Because your external world will naturally change as you change internally, you might find yourself interested in changing jobs or moving. Take a closer look. You may be ready to act on your new values and find something that is healthier for the new you.

New clothes, jobs, homes, roommates, friends, food, and leisure activities are inevitable as people develop healthier lives. Each new change takes a commitment of time and energy. Rather than focusing on the effort it will require to make the change, be motivated by what the new change means to you. It is a reflection of the hard work you have done so far. You are rewarding yourself for daring to become a healthy, whole person.

Exercise: Take time to notice your reaction to the elements of your life. Are you tired of going out to the same old smoky clubs? Are you ready to try using more or less make-up? Do you wish you had a lovely view out your window? Is your job making you unhappy? Does your choice in clothes reflect the real you? Do you feel cozy and at home where you live? The questions we might ask ourselves are endless as we grow and change. Luckily, there are plenty of inner cues that tell us when we need a change. We only have to listen regularly to our inner thoughts.

The Value Of Community

How many of us live in apartment buildings, neighborhoods, or streets surrounded by people—yet we don't know another soul? Our modern world is full of people and connected by high-tech communication devices: even so, many of us feel alone.

Today's single household has replaced a house full of many generations. In days past, our grandparents, aunts, uncles, and cousins, may have all lived together or in the same town. Now, we are lucky to talk to any of them by phone.

No One Left Alone

In extended families and small communities, no one was left alone to deal with a problem. People may have meddled too much, but advice and attention were never far away.

Today, it is easy to get up, go to work, say a few friendly hellos to fellow workers, do errands at lunch, buy food for dinner, and return home to watch television without anyone really knowing us or what is going on in our lives. This is very lonely.

Isolated Misery

Our friends are the characters we see each week in our favorite programs. We get our advice from Oprah Winfrey and Phil Donahue. We seek comfort by filling our empty loneliness with food and anything else that takes our minds temporarily off the quiet hours that stretch endlessly ahead.

No wonder we eat. This isolation is too much to handle. We have to block out our misery—and the terror that things may never change.

Most of us are social creatures by nature. We may not be extroverts, but we like the companionship of others. If given the choice, we would have a healthy dose of doing things with others on a daily basis.

Real Social Needs

For women, this social need is often even more highly developed because relationships have been important to us since the beginning of our lives. Although little boys receive socialization to direct them toward outward achievement very early on, little girls receive encouragement to connect with the people around them. Girls learn to be sensitive to the needs of others through listening and conversation and to respond to these needs. This relational focus remains highly important for most women throughout their lives.

While personal growth certainly requires discovering our untapped talents and needs, it also means honoring the things that are important and comfortable to us as well.

> *Girls learn to be sensitive to the needs of others through listening and conversation and to respond to these needs. This relational focus remains highly important for most women throughout their lives.*

Relationships—a variety of healthy, solid connections—are one of those elements that we as modern women often neglect to include in our conscious growth.

Creating A Community

Finding friends, meeting neighbors, identifying people we can call in an emotional crisis, and even lining up resources to fix our cars, water our plants when we are away, and do small household repairs—is the basis of assembling a community of people who know and support us.

Some of us take these relationships for granted. If we are lucky enough to have large families that value togetherness and we remain in their vicinity, then we may have enough people around us. But many of us today face each night alone and don't know who to call when we are really in trouble. If this is true for us—even if we seem to know a lot of people—then we need to find new and supportive people we can include in our lives.

Getting Out There

For many, finding real friends evolves from joining a support group or   social activity of some sort. It often means we have to take the first step and get ourselves out to meet people. Getting involved in something that is important to us—like an environmental, social, or neighborhood cause—will increase

the likelihood that we will cross paths with folks that have the same values as we do.

If our isolation has made us unsure of ourselves and whether anyone will like us, then taking these first steps will be monumental and very difficult. They are worth taking. Inevitably, if we involve ourselves in things we really care about, we will eventually find people we click with in these gatherings.

We may have to open ourselves up more than we are used to in order to let others get to know us. If we remain completely silent and shy, it makes it tremendously hard for people to connect with us. If opening up is hard, then certainly begin by joining a small support group to get a feeling of safety and trust as we learn to open up.

Resolving Conflict…By Listening To The Heart

We struggle all of our lives to find balance. Every day is full of conflicts that we have to resolve. Thankfully, most of the problems we have to solve are small and relatively familiar: we are hungry, but it is not time to eat; we don't know the best way to go about our new project, so we just jump in and learn as we go; or our car broke, so now we have to get it fixed within our budget and schedule.

Conflicts Of Desire

Conflicts between people are also part of everyday life. Different people want different things. If they live or work together, inevitably, these conflicting desires will create situations in which both sides cannot have exactly what they want when they want it. This can create anger, hurt, confusion, and resentment.

Depending on the nature of the relationship, the two people will talk about it or not. If they don't, the feelings go underground and fester. The problem simply keeps getting bigger and bigger until the internal pressure gets so great that something has to give. Anger flares, tears flow, feelings get hurt, and hope is bruised.

Undermining Trust

Some arguments or misunderstandings escalate to the point that neither side can hear or appreciate the other's perspective. Injurious remarks are flung about without thinking. Accusations fill the air. Distrust grows.

This can happen at home or work, with a friend or lover, or with a parent or child. Each person sees the situation from his or her point of view—which is based on the way he or she takes in daily experiences. We tend to assume that what is real or true for us is obvious to everyone. So we assume that what we see as right in any given argument

is the truth of the situation. When the other person doesn't see it that way, we feel betrayed. Our confidence in their commitment to us is undermined. We wonder if it is worth going on.

Early Impressions

Two things work against us here. The first is that each of us has gone through a unique set of circumstances that has shaped our emotional assumptions. All of our interpretations and reactions spin out from there.

For example, if a young girl grew up in a home where she never got any verbal approval or assurance about what she was

> *Every one of us has countless emotional belief patterns that color everything we experience and drive our emotional reactions. We think we see truth. We don't.*

doing, she may have a great need from the key people in her life to provide that assurance. If she doesn't get it, she feels as neglected as she did growing up. She is probably not conscious of this pattern unless she has gone through therapy. Chances are, she has depended on people in a very needy way that makes them feel burdened or repelled. She needs too much from them, so they tend to pull back.

This only makes the problem worse, and the cycle repeats itself. Each time this happens, her hurt gets deeper. She is carrying the original pain plus each new layer of rejection. Her need intensifies. She reaches out more desperately after each rebuff only to receive an even stronger rejection.

Learning From Patterns

She is looking for what she needs in the wrong place. She will not get healed by other people. Instead, she must learn from her interaction that she has a pattern of hurt which is triggered when someone pulls back from her in time of need. Then she has the opportunity to begin to work on why the pattern is there, what is missing in her life, what she needs to change, and realistic options she has for actually healing this old wound.

Every one of us has countless emotional belief patterns that color everything we experience and drive our emotional reactions. We think we see truth. We don't. We see the world through these emotional belief systems which have been deeply imprinted in our psyches. When people argue, these differing imprints affect their interpretations of the situation.

Mirroring Our Souls

Every conflict is an opportunity for us to learn about ourselves. We are getting our beliefs mirrored back to us through this person. Because every experience is filtered through our belief systems, our reactions reflect these internal beliefs. When we keep having the same kind of argument again and again, or we keep getting hurt in the same way, we have emotional beliefs that are getting us into trouble. We need to do some emotional investigation into ourselves to find out what is going on at a deeper level.

Even though the other person may be doing something hurtful or uncalled for, we have little hope of changing another person. We simply want to get out of this emotional rut we are in and attract a different kind of experience. But until we get these emotional beliefs cleared out, we will still experience the world through their limiting frameworks. Once they are actually healed and gone, they will not be part of our filtering process. Their power will be gone.

Balancing Element

When we go through life, we often bounce back and forth between feeling our emotions and thinking things through with our minds. Too often, our minds and emotions are in conflict, too. What we think we should do is not what we want to do. What we feel is right, doesn't seem right when we think about it. We can get trapped in this dilemma for a long time.

Opposites will remain opposites, so we will not be able to come to peace by either favoring our minds or our emotions. We have to find a balancing element. Our hearts can create that balance.

Possibility Of Peace

The heart wants everything and everyone to flourish. There is room for all. There is no need to see everything as black and white. There is a middle space where both sides can reside peacefully.

To get there, both sides have to acknowledge the validity of the other. Each has to allow that truth resides in the other person's perspective, too. If both sides have a valid perspective, then it is possible to find a way for both to co-exist. This is our heart's goal: to find a peaceful way for both to exist.

Compassionate Co-Existence

Our hearts ask us to get beyond our judgements of others. To make our viewpoint right, we judge the other side as more limited, stupid, dense, unclear, hysterical, and so on. We sometimes make these judgements very bluntly. We more often use a very sophisticated and subtle form of labeling and discrimination. This lets us keep up the illusion that we are broad-minded or compassionate.

Yet if we find ourselves in a struggle with someone over something, then both truths are not being allowed to co-exist. We may be part of the problem.

Sometimes, we receive judgements from others and fight to retain the right to co-exist with them. This leads us to the second element that causes great confusion in arguments.

Sex Gets In The Way

As we learn more about the psychology and physiology of men and women, we confirm just how different men are from women.

Each gender takes in experience in an extraordinarily different way. This gets us into trouble if our conflict happens to be with someone of the opposite sex—and many of them are.

Men do not and cannot really understand women based on their personal experiences. Women do not and cannot really understand men based on their personal experiences.

But men have an edge. They are given authority, power, impact, and significance merely because of their gender. Our patriarchal system perpetuates this so that men experience a world that functions like they do. Because the world is structured in such a familiar way, it never dawns on them that there is another reality.

Two Different Realities

But there is. Women live it. Women live in a world that is not structured for them. They develop sensitive relationship skills because, from the beginning of their lives, they have to make sense out of a world that is set up according to different rules than they have. They listen, absorb, reach out, adapt, analyze, and transform themselves to fit into this world. From an early age, they are acutely aware that this is necessary. In short, women feel and react differently than the males they know because of differing value systems.

Since most men are unaware of women's different experience, they do not realize that women often hear messages differently than the men intended. This creates a great, big gap between the sexes. This gap of understanding complicates most arguments and misunderstandings.

Acknowledging Our Differences

We don't realize that our differences are so major. We start with our original programming as men and women. We think we can just jump in and start talking about the issues at hand. But the issues cannot be resolved until opposing perspectives are recognized and acknowledged to each have its place in the discussion. If one side tries to bully or overpower the other, the best that can happen is that the conflict will be driven underground. It will not be resolved.

Knowing in our hearts that differences can co-exist will help us recognize how much each conflict is colored by opposite perspectives. We can strive to get these differences out on the table as quickly as possible so that the argument does not escalate into damaging territory. Then, each side must do its best to see that what the other person is saying is really true for him or her. If it is true, even if it is different, it must be taken into account as the discussion progresses. It cannot be dismissed as crazy, weak, outdated, or hysterical. It is real for that person and must be heard. When both sides are acknowledged, then there can be an honest exploration of the options for resolution.

Surviving
The Holidays

"The holidays are a time for real learning about who we are, what we want, where we come from, and where we want to go. If we examine our hopes and dreams and plan a way to get through the holidays in a manner that feels sane, whole, and renewing for ourselves, then we can have a true personal rebirth."

Surviving The Holidays

The holiday season culminates a year of growth, achievement, challenge, and pain. Traditional secular and Judeo-Christian celebrations speak of light, thanksgiving, and rebirth. Families come together, people throw parties, and business slows down. We break away from routines and prepare for another year.

Messages Of Joy And Hope

The holidays are supposed to be a time of joy. Children anticipate Hanukkah and Christmas with great excitement. Store windows, specials on television, and the music we hear are filled with messages of goodwill, peace, love, and most of all, hope for a better world.

Why then are holidays so painful for so many people? Why is there so much depression and suicide during these few weeks? Why does something that is supposed to be wonderful feel so stressful? Why can't we wait for it to be over?

For most people, the holidays are a mixture of pleasure and pain. For some, the holidays are pure pain. For individuals who struggle with food, the holidays are an especially difficult time of year to handle. At a minimum, the holidays represent a time of increased stress.

Pleasure And Pain

It is not surprising that the holidays come packaged with both pleasure and pain. We enjoy the colored lights, smell of pine, candle-lighting, special foods, and traditional rituals. We look forward to getting together with people, decorating, cooking, and buying things for people we care about.

We also may remember feelings from childhood. The holidays always seemed so magical compared to other times of the year. People bustled around. There seemed to be more fun, food, and of course, presents.

Memories Of Magic

We carry these memories and associations with us and these are what get us into trouble. We expect to feel magic. We expect people to act more joyfully and kindly toward others. We expect to feel connected and warm toward those we know and love. We expect to go to parties and feel bountiful and blessed.

The problem is that most people don't change during the holidays. Neither do our finances or our relationships. Things stay pretty much the same—except everything glitters. It is easy to feel disappointment.

> *The holidays are supposed to be a time of joy. Children anticipate Hanukkah and Christmas with great excitement. Store windows, specials on television, and the music we hear are filled with messages of good will, peace, love, and most of all, hope for a better world.*

Hollow Ring Of Holidays

After awhile, we begin to feel that the holidays are hollow: everything appears beautiful on the surface, but very little changes inside. If this is a time of thankfulness, light, and rebirth, shouldn't the holidays have a real impact on how people live? When they don't, our hurt can run deep, causing us to be bitter and cynical.

In fact, the holidays can bring out the worst in everyone. With extra demands on one's time, stress levels go up.

We have to fit in more food shopping, gatherings after work and in neighborhoods, running around to buy gifts or clothes for special occasions, traveling, and bigger bills. If our lives are already busy, we don't need this aggravation. On top of everything, there are the crowds to battle in stores and traffic on the roads. If weather is cold and stormy, it can make things downright miserable.

Families Aren't Friendly

Then there are the get-togethers. When we celebrate with family and friends, we walk in carrying all of the feelings and history we have shared with these people. Our backgrounds do not simply melt away for special occasions.

If our families are full of conflict or painful secrets, this reality lies just below the surface. Everyone tries to put troubles behind them for now by smiling, being pleasant, and acting as if nothing is wrong.

An Empty Gulf

We may choose to join in the game of pretend in which everyone "forgets" there are problems. The price we pay for this choice is a feeling of being fake. The whole gathering seems full of false concern and love. This is very lonely and painful. But expressing real feelings creates too much turbulence for everyone

The gulf between family members or friends is often felt most acutely during holidays because we are supposed to feel so much closeness. If families or friends do not know how to share feelings and problems, then the distance between people may be extra painful. This can cause increased depression, stress, and even suicides.

Food Everywhere

And finally, there is food everywhere. People bake and bring things to the office. There are parties. Candy dishes are full. Stores are filled with smells of carmel, baked goods, chocolate, and cinnamon.

Holidays meals themselves are usually quite a production—with more food than anyone could or should ever eat. There are high fat, high calorie, and wonderfully delicious cookies, breads, desserts, gravies, and dishes seen only once a year.

We want to taste every one of these special, delicious foods. We want to indulge

ourselves and feel the joy and celebration that pure pleasure brings.

Innocent Indulging

We don't want to have to think about diets, calories, and taboos during this time of year. It seems wrong somehow that we should have to struggle with what we eat when life is supposed to be a celebration.

These foods aren't around that often anyway. They come packaged with memories of grandma and simpler times. They make us feel warm and special—that life can be simple and easy.

We remember things from our childhoods and touch the innocence we once knew. We want that back. It is hard to be grown up.

The holidays, with all of the food and celebrations, can make us feel young again. We like this feeling. So we play, indulge, eat, and often pay for it later by beating ourselves up.

Recognize The Conflict

So what can we do to survive? We can sort out what the holidays mean to us. Then we can figure out what we can do to get through this time of stress in a way that will be healthier for us.

Exercise: *Recognizing that there are aspects which may create both positive and negative feelings or reactions is an important first step to surviving the holidays. If you dread the holidays, you are not crazy. If you look forward to the holidays every year, but feel a little empty afterward, this makes sense.*

Start a holiday section of your journal and write about your memories of holidays past. Focus on specific events, people, and feelings. Write about holidays that you remember as a child, adolescent, and adult. Reasons for your reactions to this season will begin to surface.

Renewing Ourselves

There are very few occasions or events which offer us the chance to replenish ourselves in this rush, rush society. The holidays can be a time for personal renewal if we can survive the stress that come with them.

The holidays give us an atmosphere which reminds us that we are on a journey for deeper meaning. If we take the time to look beyond the glitter and into our deeper selves, we may find that the holidays help us develop the spiritual sides of our lives.

Connecting With A Higher Power

In earlier decades, religious life performed this function. Once a week, a person attended church or synagogue to turn the attention away from worldly affairs. One's focus went inward and upward instead, connecting the individual with a higher being, purpose, or power.

This weekly practice still is meaningful for many people. However, religion plays a less central role in many people's lives. For some, this lack of spiritual focus leaves them without a way to make sense of the inevitable struggles that come with living.

Lack of Meaning

Many have tried to fill this void with achievement. The pursuit of careers, material possessions, glamourous travel, nightlife, and addictions of all sorts including work, food, alcohol, drugs, sex, etc, have served as a replacement for inner life.

But none of these things work. An emptiness remains because what we really need as human beings is meaning and purpose. We need to make sense out of life. We need to know why things happen the way they do.

We need ultimately to make peace with the course of our own lives and find inner happiness.

Making Sense Of Our Lives

The answers to these big questions never lie outside ourselves. They come from within. Traditionally, religion provided answers. But if the traditions in which you were raised do not give you a sense of meaning, then you have to find answers for yourself. You will find insight, guidance, and comfort in unexpected places—from people, places, books, journaling, and daily events.

Knowing that you are on a personal quest helps. You are gathering resources. Comfort and meaning are not going to be handed to

> *The holidays give us an atmosphere which reminds us that we are on a journey for deeper meaning. If we take the time to look beyond the glitter and into our deeper selves, we may find that the holidays help us develop the spiritual side of our lives.*

you in one ready-made package. It may take a while to work this out for yourself. But there is no rush.

Using The Holidays

The holiday season or festivities may provide you with an opportunity to explore your inner spirit. Through simple contacts with people, the act of giving or being kind to another, taking time for refection on your life and how it is evolving, you may find you are enhanced or renewed.

Renewal means to make new again…to capture a moment of the clean energy and fresh attitude we feel when we begin something. Usually we feel hope and anticipation at the start of something new. We are optimistic and feel that anything is possible.

Renewing Ourselves

Somewhere along the way we get tired and jaded. We need to be replenished—to have our hope and optimism renewed and to have our faith in our deepest selves and others refreshed because we have been bruised.

The holidays can refresh us if we let go of unrealistic images of complete togetherness and joy. If we look instead for what things we can learn about ourselves and what things we can offer to make this a better world, we may find our inner spirits reawakened. The potential for this kind of personal rebirth is especially powerful during holidays.

Exercise: *Find a quiet place to sit and think. If you can, pick a place that makes you feel part of something larger—a cathedral, ocean shore, beautiful horizon, or a stairway in the dark.*

Think about everything that has happened this past year. Acknowledge how you have grown. Think about how you hope to change in the coming year. Ask yourself what the real purpose is to your life. Then ask if there is anything you need to do in the next few weeks to complete this year's lessons. Is there anything that could connect you to your higher purpose? Very gently and privately, follow these inner thoughts to renew yourself.

Holiday Dread: Out Of Control With Food

*H*ave you ever dieted before the holidays because you know you will eat more than normal? Do you think that gaining weight is inevitable during the holidays? Do you find yourself on crash diets after the holidays are over, painfully trying to peel off the pounds that accumulated so quickly in the last few weeks? Do you dread holidays and food?

Hardest Time Of Year

You are not alone. For individuals who struggle with food, whether they are compulsive eaters, overeaters, anorexics, or bulimics, the holidays are the hardest time of year. Although family strain and disappointed hopes are part of why holidays are hard, the fear of food plays a main role.

Food seems to be everywhere. It is unavoidable. Ordinary, everyday eating seems hard enough to control without all of the extra temptations of the holidays. With special sweets, party foods, and traditional holiday dishes, sanity feels impossible. Moderation is out of the question. Control vanishes and shame sets in.

Control Breaks Down

If we are out of control with our eating, it is natural to assume that having more control will fix the problem. So we focus on control mechanisms—dieting, restricting, taboo foods, avoiding food-related events, keeping binge foods out of the house, skipping meals, distraction techniques—anything to not give in and eat.

Control mechanisms are bound to fail at least some of the time for two reasons: it is impossible to control all of the factors surrounding food, and we are eating for a reason. Until we recognize why we are eating—what is motivating us to eat—we will not have control.

Hidden Needs

If we begin to deal with the underlying reasons for eating and develop alternatives for coping with these problems other than food, then it won't be so hard to be around food.

If we have not dealt with any of the underlying pain that drives us to eat, the holidays will probably be a disaster for us. Even if we are successful at restricting our access or reactions to food, if we really want to eat, then we set ourselves up for later binges.

The Holiday Challenge

So what can we do? How can we get through the holidays without feeling scared of or controlled by food?

> *W*ith special sweets, party foods, and traditional holiday dishes, sanity seems impossible. Moderation is out of the question. Control vanishes and shame sets in.

The most important thing to do to get ready is to pay attention to our feelings. Our urges to eat are often a reflection of how much conflict or pain we are feeling.

Our attraction to food is a wonderful barometer of pain and emotional health because it has become our coping mechanism. We eat to cope, not to fuel the body. So if we are overeating, most likely we are coping with some stressful feelings.

Eating Measures Stress

We may not be aware of the feelings because we use food to block them out. But if we begin to see the connection, we can then work to find out what is really bothering us.

This is not easy, and it may require finding a therapist who can help you. It may be too hard to face the pain alone. Usually, the stresses we are dealing with are quite painful or we would not want or need to hide them.

This process of personal insight can be done all year round. Since holidays are filled with emotional conflict—family disappointments, loneliness, and financial strain—our eating may increase because our need to cope increases. This is what really drives our excessive eating. So identifying and dealing with feelings is crucial now.

Exercise: *Notice what you are really hungry for. Let yourself taste the foods you want to taste. Notice if they taste as fabulous as you imagined. Stop if they aren't as good as you thought. If they are great, enjoy them. Try to eat when you are hungry and not just because food is there. If you are at a party, wait until your body is physically hungry.*

At holiday meals, try everything you want, but take smaller portions. Often special meals cause people to pile plates high and take extra helpings. Eat what you like, but in a quantity that is respectful to your body and matches the level of your real hunger.

Resist urgings from family members to eat for their pleasure (I made this just for you!) Respond with gratitude and tell them you'll be delighted to have some when you are hungry.

Decide what is best for you and your body. Eat on your own schedule as much as possible. Allow yourself to eat when you are hungry. Allow yourself to fulfill your desires—taste what you want and eat what you like. Listen to your body to judge appropriate quantities. It knows when it is full.

If you find yourself overeating, walk outside for a minute and ask yourself what is wrong. This is probably a signal that something is bothering you.

If you realize you are dealing with a painful feeling or reaction to the situation, promise yourself that you will deal with it. If you can, go back and do or say something.

If not, make sure you honor your promise to yourself by writing in your journal, crying, or talking to your therapist or someone else later. If you really follow through on your commitment to deal with the feeling, you will begin to trust yourself. Your inner self knows it can trust that you will take care of it. The power of food will begin to be lessened.

The Secret Pain Of Family Gatherings

*I*f being with your family of origin (parents, siblings, and others) is a joyful, uplifting experience that you look forward to, then you are blessed with a naturally supportive family system.

Many people do not experience their families in this easy, loving way. Going home is awkward and maybe even painful. They are returning to families that are dysfunctional—not able to function as a healthy whole. This is part of the extra stress of the holidays.

Dysfunctional Families

Family members in dysfunctional families have trouble expressing their individualities. More energy is spent on maintaining a perfect exterior than on recognizing the unique characteristics and growth of each member.

This means that there are all kinds of unspoken rules that people have to follow or others will get upset. Most of the rules protect people from the truth because the truth would be too upsetting.

So going home at the holidays means returning to a place where you were never recognized for who you were. Going home means having to turn yourself and your feelings off if you do not want to cause trouble. Going home means feeling invisible and isolated. Going home feels lonely.

Invisible Rules

It may be hard to identify this at first because everything seems fine on the surface. People are together—laughing, talking, and getting things ready. But something is missing.

No one talks about the divorce that just happened and how everyone is feeling. No one comments on how much drinking is going on. Everyone acts as if the cruel comment that is made wasn't said or didn't hurt.

If someone dares to comment, disagree, or stand up to the offender, she is met with silence. No one else backs her up. She knows she is right and that everyone else agrees, but she is left to battle alone. She becomes the black sheep for daring to question the family.

An Unhealthy Peace

Very quickly, people learn to conform. They must to stay in the system. Others choose to leave and no one ever understands why.

The ones who stay may end up acting out the unhealthiness by getting unhealthy themselves. They may develop illnesses,

> *I*f a person uses food to hide feelings, she will find herself eating more than she wants. She needs to eat to keep the lid on.

addictions, behavior problems, emotional disorders, abusive tendencies toward themselves or others, and so on. The tension has to be acted out.

It may be verbally denied, but the underlying reality remains. The family that desperately wants to have everything be fine is in pain underneath.

Personal Cover-Ups

The unspoken feelings build up inside and trigger another cover up because they cannot be expressed in this environment. If a person uses food to hide feelings, she will find herself eating more than she wants. She needs to eat to keep the lid on.

Others do this by drinking, having fits of anger, getting headaches, being peacemakers, sleeping, etc. Everyone plays a different role in the family, but each works out a way to cover up feelings that are not allowed.

This dampens the joy and connectedness everyone wants to feel during the holidays.

The Holidays Are Here Again

The strain of the holidays is often not openly acknowledged. We are supposed to feel alive and full of magic. Our hearts should be full. We should feel grateful for all that we have, and ready to share our abundant feelings with the world.

When reality doesn't measure up to the images we have absorbed since childhood, we assume something must be wrong with us. We must be "scrooges" for feeling overwhelmed or negative.

Added Stress

The reality is that the holidays are the most stressful time of year—without dispute! The added demands of shopping are grueling. Finding the money to pay for gifts and buy new outfits can throw budgets into a tailspin

If we aren't true to ourselves and our feelings, we set ourselves up for depression. We will feel so alone.

that might take months to repair. Feeling obligated to throw parties or coordinate family events can add more financial and emotional strain.

Having to act like we are happy and have our lives together when we see people, is another struggle. The energy it takes to fake our way through the inevitable multitude of questions, stories, comparisons, and so on is enormous. We could be honest about what our lives are really like, but who wants to throw a damper over the good cheer that seems to abound everywhere we go?

Seven Pounds Per Holiday

Because the thought of all the food that waits ahead is also terrifying, we decide to try and lose a few pounds before the festivities begin.

Stressful? Absolutely. It wouldn't matter so much if we just didn't care. If we could turn our backs and ignore all of the goings-on, it wouldn't be so hard.

Childhood Dreams Still Alive

The truth is, the holidays are special to us. Even if our childhood memories are not all rosy, the promise of hope and love became ingrained into our personal mythology. Part of us wished that all of the wonder could become real.

We fervently wanted peace—in our world, at home, and inside our selves. We wished to give love and feel it in return. We wished for a better world and a better life. We saw people acting happier and more joyful than usual, and we hoped that things would be different from now on.

Darkness And Light

But there was an undercurrent of darkness. Mama and papa were moody. There was more drinking than usual. Strain caused tempers to let loose. People fought. Bills mounted up. Everyone was busy and tired.

Holidays were time for goodwill, but everyone rushed around trying to get everything done. It didn't fit together. The messages were confusing. People were full of joy, but then they argued. It was a time for rebirth and hope, but no one had time to reflect on their lives and their world.

An Issue Of Trust

Not surprisingly, this kind of confusion makes us cautious. What is true? Is the love everyone talks about real?

How do we protect ourselves from the stress we sense everywhere? Is it even right that we are thinking about self-protection when we are supposed to be open and sharing love with the world?

And why are we so concerned with our images during a time when our souls are supposed to be most important? Instead, it's our clothes, our hair, and our weight that everyone notices. Isn't this just a little bit crazy?

Holiday Hatred

We eat when we are confused, so now we have a real reason to hate the holidays: they make us eat—not just because there is a lot of food around—but because we are feeling so stressed. If we try to figure this whole thing out philosophically, we find ourselves eating out of frustration!

So we give up and just try to get through. Sometimes that means avoiding food— or certain people, places, or gatherings. Sometimes we pretend just like everyone else does. Or we might even isolate ourselves until after the whole thing is over.

Being True To Our Dreams

If we aren't true to ourselves and our feelings, we set ourselves up for depression. We feel so alone.

Even though things around us may feel false, unreal, and disconnected, we don't have to do the same thing ourselves.

We can choose to be honest, loving, and nurturing to ourselves during this time. We can make the holidays special and full of promise for ourselves. We can seek to live more peacefully and gently even if others do not.

We need to take time to think about what is important to us and how we are going to handle our holiday obligations in a way that feels congruent with our values.

Some events we may skip. We may schedule an alternative time and place to see the people we care about. We may act more low-key than others expect of us. We may stay sober and really observe what happens.

Permission To Grow

The holidays give us permission to be more alive and hopeful than other times of the year. They hold the promise of rebirth. The lights, smells, and music help us get in touch with softer sides of ourselves.

Taking time during the holidays to evaluate who we are and what we really value for the coming year can be very powerful. The glamour and glitter will be gone as soon as this season passes, but our growth will continue.

A personal promise for growth and nurturing will remain a steadfast beacon of inner light that guides us the rest of the year.

Exercise: *Find some private time one evening. Light candles and play your favorite holiday music. Fix yourself some tea, eggnog, cocoa, or warm milk with cinnamon and honey. Settle into a comfortable chair with paper and pen or your journal. Begin to write about the true meaning of the holidays for yourself and what inspires you about this time. Write about your life and the hopes you have for yourself. Write about the promises you can make for yourself and the coming year. Be loving and gentle as you think about what is really possible.*

The Return To Innocence

As we learn to be whole people, many of us often discover that our hearts have been broken in the past. As a consequence, we learned to put up shields and protect them from ever getting hurt again. Nothing or no one would ever make us feel so small or unloved.

Focus On Success

Instead, we focused on being successful. We got busy. We made good grades, found good jobs, and looked like we had everything together. On the outside, maybe we did. On the inside, we were still shattered.

Our achievement was supposed to make up for the sense of worthlessness and abandon which we felt after our original

As we heal, we discover that we cannot be whole unless we add back our wonder, awe, innocence, play, delight, joy, and spontaneity into our lives.

heartbreak, but it never really worked. Inside, we were still hurt.

Our hurt made us grow up fast and give up our sense of awe and wonder at the world. We gave up playing early because we had become responsible. We also gave up our fantasies because they would never come true in this kind of a world.

Wide-Eyed Wonder

As we heal, we discover that we cannot be whole unless we add back our wonder, awe, innocence, play, delight, joy, and spontaneity into our lives.

Living is about discovery. As babies, we loved to find out new things every single day. Every new sight was inspiring and delightful. This same innocent, exploring spirit is still inside waiting to lead us forward in our lives.

Innocence means taking in an experience without judging it. We need to learn to be in an experience and be open to what it has to teach us. We need to let it unfold magically and mysteriously in its own way.

This is the wide-eyed, open-mouthed wonder of the child. If we judge something first, we are guessing at truth rather than allowing it to unfold. Therefore, we limit any experience's potential to impact our lives. We are more likely to remain stuck because we don't let in anything new.

The holidays are a great time for remembering and practicing innocence. There are many moments where we can pause and look at the colored lights, listen to the music wafting over us, enjoy the delight of a child, and extend a hand to someone who needs a kind gesture.

We can observe and absorb without judging. We can simply enjoy and let the beauty fill our hearts and soul. Every small moment counts. Allowing ourselves to be innocent during the holidays will make us better at noticing and absorbing wonder the rest of the year.

Exercise: *Remember your most special memory or favorite part of the holidays. Figure out a way to add it back into your life. Do it with/for yourself, a child, or loved one.*

Making Peace With Family Ghosts

Holidays and family gatherings always go together. If our healing and development involves making peace with food, then family issues are surely involved.

Painful Pasts

Chances are, we have had to deal with difficult feelings about our families. Coming face to face with people who have played important and too often traumatic roles in our lives can be hard.

Family pain is as common as personal pain—because families are made up of individuals who are struggling with current problems and painful pasts.

Family pain can be as simple as the members not talking to each other about what is really happening inside. A parent might live too heavily through a child's life—or maintain emotional distance to avoid getting hurt.

Parents might turn to alcohol or drugs to numb their pain. They might act out their fear and frustration through violent tempers or abuse.

When people have children, they can only act from the experience that shaped them. If their treatment as children was not healthy, often this same pattern is repeated, and the pain is passed on.

The parents' behaviors structure the life patterns of their children who in turn act out a variation of the same theme. The pattern is stopped only when someone actively and consciously chooses to get help.

In a therapeutic process, early family experiences are often remembered. The feelings they caused come back and are felt deeply. This is not easy to do.

Truth Exposed

If a family gathering occurs during this kind of work, it can leave a person feeling raw and exposed. She has uncovered the truth about the family, and it hurts. Being with the people associated with the hurt can cause fresh pain.

It also can be verifying. Once you see your family for what it is—a collection of people who have their own strengths and shortcomings due to their upbringings—being with family is like doing an experiment: you can gather data and see how things really work firsthand.

Often there is current evidence of the same behaviors that have hurt you in the past. This does wonders for dispelling doubts: it is normal to wonder whether you made up your memories or are exaggerating what happened.

> *Being with family provides new clues to help you understand the picture even better. The clues may be your own emotional reactions, or they may be the behaviors or reactions of others.*

New Clues

Being with family provides new clues to help you understand the picture even better. The clues may be your own emotional reactions, or they may be the behaviors or reactions of others.

You will not change your family. People change only when they are ready (no one could talk you into changing until you were ready!). It is also not very helpful or healing to blame others. They have their own struggles.

Instead, you can learn to let go of the pain just enough to freely live your life now and in the future.

Going Home To Learn Again

When we find ourselves first turning inside to uncover the emotional connections we have to food, we may not yet have a glimmer that our early upbringing and family rules and relationships had an important influence on how we feel today.

As time goes by, we pursue a therapeutic process to heal our lack of self-esteem, our bruised hearts, and hidden souls. Whatever form that process takes, it usually leads us home. We return to our childhoods to remember our early reactions to events and people who were significant. We find these formed our baseline impressions of the rules about how life operates and what our role is supposed to be.

> *We return to our childhoods to remember our early reactions to events and people who were significant. We find these formed our baseline impressions of the rules about how life operates and what our role is supposed to be.*

Long Time Healing

Often these childhood interpretations and conclusions—which made sense to us at the time since our vision and experience were still so limited—carry over into our thinking and behavior as adults. As we dig, we find that the childhood belief systems and emotional conclusions are still as real today as they were then.

We spend a long time healing these wounds. We make our peace—and find we now can make new choices. We can re-interpret the beliefs that were formed so long ago. This helps us feel like real adults. Although there is still a lot of growing to do, our lives are beginning to feel like our own.

And then we go home for the holidays. In a matter of minutes it seems, we find ourselves back in the old system. It barely matters that we have done all of this personal hard work. The rest of our family is caught in a time warp. Nothing has changed.

Returning To The Past

And so regardless of how we work to bring our new limits, boundaries, insights, and interpretations home with us, we find ourselves triggered into emotional reactions that feel like the same old stuff.

It is the same old stuff—yet it is not. Since the rest of the family has not gone through a rebirth of understanding, they have no reason to change. Everything they say or do comes from their internal emotional patterns which have never had a chance to heal. They expect us to fit into the same roles and places we have always taken because this is how the family works. So what we experience actually is the same.

But we are different inside. We no longer can innocently and unknowingly adopt our old roles. We may wish we could because our new selves are not as accepted. People don't like us speaking our minds…not joining in with the drinking and rowdiness…leaving when something feels abusive… asking for what we need… or reacting with real emotion when we are hurt or angry.

On Shaky Ground

We are disrupting the status quo—and everyone is on shaky ground until things get back to normal. We experience enormous pressure to fit in and quit making trouble.

Unfortunately, we cannot return to our old ways because we would be hurting ourselves. It is no longer an option since it is our inner selves which stick with us through thick and thin. We find it is more important to honor our own needs than try to please others at our own expense.

Yet we find ourselves feeling so raw. Now that we are aware of our inner feelings and personal pain, when something hurtful is said, we feel it. We now perceive the neglect we once accepted as normal. We recognize our friends' and family's need to anesthetize pain with drinking, food, and superficial conversation—which we once took for having a good time.

Gathering Clues

It is not easy going home. Yet if we stay awake and don't succumb to the same need to cover things over, we will experience our true feelings and reactions at a deeper level than ever before. We will be triggered by these behaviors in new ways. We will see new aspects of the patterns that we never noticed before. We will get clearer insight on our roles with these people—and how this carries over into our daily lives. With each interaction, we will feel the emotions more deeply and honestly that these relationships create in us.

This is a wonderful opportunity! It is like going to school—emotional school! Where else will we experience such a rich and personalized set of relationships that can trigger our emotions so perfectly? How else can we really get to know the inner makeup that is uniquely ours?

Going home with the intention to learn about our family dynamics, where we fit in, and how our personal emotional systems have gotten structured in response can help get us through the difficulties of actually being there.

It also helps remind us of how far we've come and that we are choosing to do this emotional work. We want to recover and heal—and it is almost impossible without transforming the childhood interpretations of our experience.

Survival Strategies

So go home this holiday season with anticipation rather than dread. Yes, you may feel drained afterward. Make sure you have some support strategies to get you through—continue to see your therapist; keep a journal so you can go back and remember what got triggered and why; arrange for friends to be available by phone who will lend you moral support; make sure you take a breather now and again by going for a walk or running an errand; or schedule time to replenish yourself with a hot bath or daytime nap. Taking care of yourself throughout this challenging growth period is essential to not getting overwhelmed.

Afterward, take time to reflect on what you saw, felt, and heard. This new information may fuel your therapeutic work for months to come. As you continue to heal, your presence in your family will be increasingly different than what they expect. As you get stronger, you may find that some of these relationships actually begin to shift. As you are more honest and open, some of your family might begin to open up, too. What at first seemed like choice to keep you outside the family structure, eventually can help you find a place more honestly inside of it. Your family may never change to your liking. There still may be plenty of deception and covering over of real feelings. But you may find a way to authentically bring yourself back inside this important group of people in your life.

Finding Joy

For a person who has been through a lifetime of tough experiences, joy is one of the last qualities to return. It is a natural outgrowth of the healing process, but it may come later rather than earlier.

Joy can begin to present itself in tiny glimpses almost right away when we undertake healing journeys. The release that comes from gaining new perspectives on our pain and redefine ourselves in new ways can be very exhilarating. After new realizations, we may find ourselves laughing or enjoying our surroundings spontaneously.

The First Taste

These first moments of joy are very important because they give us a taste of what is possible in our everyday lives. This

Joy is just as healing as all the hard work we do on our inner selves. We desperately need moments of simple delight to restore our faith in the healing power of nature.

positive feeling of freedom will not stay. Inevitably our growth will take us back into our psychic muck to continue cleaning up. We go back into darkness, heaviness, hurt, and hopelessness, until we again surface with a new layer of understanding and release.

Moments of joy and peace in between our intense processing become precious indeed. They are small spaces in which we can become childlike again. We can simply enjoy the sun and sky and earth for what it is. Small children or birdsongs give us great delight. A melody on the radio fills us with incredible content.

Healing Moments

Joy is just as healing as all the hard work we do on our inner selves. We desperately need moments of simple delight to restore our faith in the healing power of nature. If we don't believe there is a chance to heal, then why undergo the immense pain of looking at all our inner personal garbage? We need joy to prove that life can truly be aligned again with hope, love, and fullness—rather than hatred, cruelty, and pain.

As we heal, we learn to make more space for joy in our lives. By noticing the natural rhythms in healing—diving into inner memories and beliefs and then coming out to try on these new perspectives for awhile. The inner dive is never fun at the bottom and may seem unending. The breathing space we get in between these dives seems so short in comparison. But the cycle keeps repeating itself—and it will as long as we continue on our journey. By letting ourselves fully enjoy the quiet times in between, we rekindle our souls' deepest faith in the journey of life.

Making Space For Joy

When a breather comes, be ready to do simple, joyful things. Go watch the waterfall. Take a walk where you can see dogs romping and babies toddling. Visit the monkeys at the zoo. Lay outside in the backyard and watch the stars. Do things that kids do. Kids haven't had all of the spontaneous silliness and delight in fooling around conditioned out of them yet. We can learn a lot from them.

Moments of joy are small celebrations of our growth. Human culture around the world recognizes the importance of practicing joy by making a big deal out of special celebrations. In our predominantly Judeo-Christian culture, the end of each year brings Hanukkah and Christmas which our society celebrates with zeal.

Rebirth And Renewal

The year-end holidays have a spiritual and metaphorical meaning of rebirth and renewal. We have time to slow down and reflect on the past year and our lives as a whole. We come together with others, make personal pledges for change, and simply live in an atmosphere of more celebration and joy than any other period throughout the year.

While holidays bring stress and potential reminders of childhood or family pain, they also present each of us with the private opportunity for joy. We can allow our more innocent, playful, and shy sides of our beings to peek out. We can stick out our tongues and catch snowflakes...fill a room with lighted candles...buy tiny presents for ourselves...and no one will question our sanity! Best of all, we won't feel self-conscious about it either.

Finding joy means trusting the process of our lives. We are on a path of growth which is taking us inward and outward—inward to heal our hearts and souls and outward to help us create lives that fit our needs. Joy comes along as we learn to accept and express our real selves.

Seven Pounds Of Dread

Each and every year, the holidays roll around again bringing cookies, candy, sweetbreads, chocolates, family feasts, party foods, and goodies at every turn. We look forward to the special foods that arrive this season and relish the opportunity to indulge our taste buds without normal restraint.

We live in fear of the mounting pounds that unrestrained eating inevitably brings—along with self-hatred, punishment, and shame. We know that most of us gain weight this time of year. The average American puts on seven pounds. For most women, seven pounds is nothing to shrug at—it is hard to diet it off and it certainly affects the way our waistbands feel when we get dressed!

> *We live in fear of the mounting pounds that unrestrained eating inevitably brings—along with self-hatred, punishment, and shame.*

Balancing The Craziness

How can we possibly balance the desire to eat holiday goodies without gaining weight? People try all sorts of things. Some are already on diets trying to lose five to 10 pounds before the holidays come. Some skip regular meals and just eat at celebrations. Some quit eating altogether to avoid the conflict. Some throw up their hands and decide to deal with it afterward.

None of this makes much sense. We know our bodies get used to a particular amount of food and activity. When we increase the food disproportionately, we gain weight. It's very simple. Trying to modulate the weight gain with periods of restriction only confuses our poor metabolisms which are already whacked out with years of dieting.

Nutritionists tell us that sensible weight management is based on consistent, regular, well-balanced meals together with leading an active lifestyle. These principles don't stop just because the holidays are here.

Because we are so busy during this season, we probably have to work a little harder at getting in our daily walks or bike rides and eating healthy, regular meals. Eating on the run makes us more susceptible to nibbling and impulsive food choices. Skipping meals makes us hungrier. Restricting makes us rebellious. So we are really working against our purpose if we begin to fool around with our eating patterns in hope of preventing weight gain.

No More Taboos

Holiday feasting certainly involves greater quantities of food than our bodies need. Food is in front of us when we are not hungry, and we are expected to eat to share camaraderie with others. But we can still follow the lessons we've learned about asking ourselves if we are really hungry and for what. Then we can feed ourselves appropriately from the foods around us and still feel in control of our choices.

This includes allowing ourselves to have portions of special food we love this time of year. Maybe we only have a bite or a small portion. If we allow ourselves to taste what we really want to taste, then we will be less likely to binge on any one thing.

Retaining Control

This also assumes that we have other means for handling the stresses we face this season. We are going to be brimming with emotions this time of year—whether we are feeling hassled by all that we have to accomplish, feeling overwhelmed at being with family again, or pressured by making good impressions at social gatherings. This is the season which accelerates emotional turmoil—which in turn accelerates eating. We must get our support system in place to help us sort out our feelings and figure out sane ways to get through the challenges before us.

Planning Ahead

Getting through crazy times can sometimes be overwhelming. If the amount we have to accomplish cranks up enormously—which often happens at the end of the year with holidays—our peace of mind and sanity is jeopardized.

We can have one of two strategies—get through the demanding times crisis by crisis or try to gain some control for ourselves by planning ahead.

Crisis By Crisis

We have all tried crisis management as a way of doing things. As we awaken each day and remember what we have to do, we panic. Every minute of the day we feel whipped by the pressure. Our bodies are in high gear all the time and our minds can barely keep everything straight. We land in bed completely fatigued—and then are up all night worrying about what we have to do tomorrow!

Inevitably, we forget important things we have to do. All of a sudden, deadlines are upon us. We never had time to figure out how we were going to get everything done, and now there's no time left. We feel like failures. Like we are barely surviving. Like we can't wait for this to be over. Like we are in hell.

The Joy Is Gone

This is no way to live. We are not having any fun, and everyone around us feels our tension. Our health suffers and we certainly do not feel the joy of the season. What's more, we feel like victims of circumstance.

Our helplessness and fatigue make us want to escape—and we do so with food. We make ourselves warm, soothing snacks. We treat ourselves to sweets to give ourselves a break from all the pressure.

Learning From The Past

Every year, it's the same. The holidays seem to hit all at once and there is too little time to get everything done. The craziness takes too much of the joy out, and everyone suffers.

There must be another way. If we look back once the pressure is over, we realize that we had another choice. We could have started preparing earlier and tried to plan ahead.

Getting ready for any high-stress period—and the holidays rank near the top of the list—takes some foresight. We have to creatively figure out how to double the amount we get done within a budget we can afford.

> *O*ur helplessness and fatigue make us want to escape—and we do so with food. We make ourselves warm, soothing snacks. We treat ourselves to sweets to give ourselves a break from all the pressure.

Holiday Hassle

Besides the pressures of shopping, cooking, decorating, correspondence, and special events, our regular routines get thrown to the wind. We sacrifice sleep, exercise, and private time—our precious rejuvenating and replenishing time.

So our internal batteries run low leaving us with less resistance to stress, illness, and unexpected changes in plans. Yet this is when we need more—not less—personal energy. Without rest, our willingness and ability to persevere evaporate in direct proportion to our fatigue.

We are in serious need of a different strategy to get us through holiday hassles.

Time and organization are key. We need to get going on things earlier and have plans that can help us keep focused.

This doesn't mean that we can't be spontaneous and enjoy the child-like quality of the holidays. To the contrary! We can enjoy ourselves much more and express our playfulness when we don't feel stretched to the maximum.

Make A Plan

When we know a big event is coming that is going to require extraordinary energy, the earlier we can take time to think through everything that is involved, the better. Writing everything down in an inventory of things to accomplish is the next step. Once we know the scope of what we have to do, we can pull out our calendars and figure out what we can do right away and what has to wait until later. If we split what we have to do over several weeks or even months, then no one day, weekend, or week will get insanely crazy.

This might mean keeping an eye out for an outfit or gifts in late summer or early fall—rather than waiting to start shopping until the day after Thanksgiving or even Christmas Eve. It is also easy begin preparing holiday cards and correspondence early, too. Party planning, filling out invitations, saving extra money, gift wrapping, etc. can all be done early. For those actual activities that have to wait—cooking, decorating, visiting friends and relatives, etc—it is especially important to think through what can realistically get done each day or week.

The holiday season is a highly emotional time. It can trigger old memories, highlight deficiencies in our lives, strain our relationship skills, and bring out our hopes and dreams.

By organizing our activities so that we are not so strained, we will not self-destruct during this very special season.

Assessing Our Needs

*S*tress comes in many forms. One of the most common types of stress, which is especially prevalent during the holidays, is caused by situations not meeting or conflicting with your needs.

You are a unique person with your own set of likes and dislikes. You have been through a unique set of circumstances and have a history of reactions which are yours alone. For your personal growth, you require certain kinds of stimulation and support which are likely to be quite different than what other people need.

It makes sense that each of us needs different kinds of support, but putting this concept into action is often quite difficult.

The Need To Belong

Many people feel an intense need to belong. Most people interpret belonging as being the same as others in the group to which you wish to belong. In other words, if you want to be part of a group, you have to be like the other members of the group.

This unspoken rule ties together ethnic groups, neighborhoods, families, departments at work, religious congregations, circles of friends, roommates, etc. Anything different feels foreign and therefore uncomfortable. Most of the time, the group does not warmly welcome individuals who do not fit the group's image or norm.

Being The Same

This principle is clearly operating in our society around the issue of body image. What is "in" today is a thin, fit, well-dressed, and beautiful body. Anything else is second-rate. The more outside this norm, the more ridicule and isolation an individual feels. This is why it is hard to be fat in America.

But this principle also operates in families at the holidays and in every social situation. If others are drinking, it is hard to abstain. If family dinner is at 8:00 but you are starved by 6:00, you probably end up eating twice. When holidays mean an abundance of tempting foods, you may have no way of moderating the menu without hurting someone else's feelings.

Standing Up For Our Needs

Most of us succumb in these situations. We do not have the guts or the fortitude to stand up for what is healthiest for us.

This is understandable. It means swimming upstream. At the very least, we are likely to confuse people. Probably, we will actually make someone angry if we buck tradition.

> *S*eeking something new is hard. Because it is unfamiliar, it is uncomfortable. It takes time to adjust, and part of that adjustment is grieving the loss of the old.

We might even be subjected to emotional isolation and punishment if we really ask to do something different than others expect.

We have to ask ourselves who are we living for? Are we on this planet to make others happy regardless of the cost to our own happiness? We might have to choose not to eat certain foods, be at certain meals, or come to particular gatherings, even though it disappoints someone else.

The Fear Of Hurting Others

If your mother, father, grandmother, and others get satisfaction or meaning through your achievements and reactions, they may feel like you are rejecting them when you reject their food or traditions.

As you figure out how to handle the holidays for yourself, you may need to let key people know that you are not rejecting them personally. You are just taking care of yourself. You still care for them and appreciate their wonderful intentions. But you need something else right now—including their understanding and acceptance.

Loneliness Of Being Different

Finally, if you make non-traditional choices during the holidays, you may have a new set of feelings to deal with. You may feel proud and grateful for your courage to request something different and then act upon it.

You may also find yourself missing the very tradition you decided was not best for you this year. You may feel sad and not know why.

When we leave things, there is often a sorrow at parting from the familiar. This sadness signals a change, a loss of the old. Familiar things, even if they are not healthy, are most comfortable.

Seeking something new is hard. Because it is unfamiliar, it is uncomfortable. It takes time to adjust, and part of that adjustment is grieving the loss of the old.

We may know definitely that we do not want to turn back, but still we feel sad at having to move on and disrupt the old order.

As you examine what feels healthy for you, you can begin to establish your own tradition and meaning for the holidays. Most likely it will include some—if not most—of the traditions that you have done for years. Chances are, it will also include some new things that feel good to you.

Exercise: *Make a list of your favorite activities associated with the holidays. Try to do as many of them as possible this year. Identify the things that are uncomfortable for you. Can you figure out why? What could you do to make it different? List several options so you have a better chance of finding one that fits both your needs and those of the people who will be affected as you make changes.*

Lost In A Box
Of Chocolates

"*The unfolding of her self-awareness and personal power occurs in layers. It is a slow and magnificent process. Over time, every corner of her being receives the light and loving attention of this personal growth process. She is waking from a living slumber. She is finding her Self.*"

Today, in our society, issues of weight, body image, and eating affect millions of people. Countless numbers of us have learned to comfort ourselves with food. We reach for food in times of stress. When our racing hearts and restless minds urge us to feel the feelings that tumble and twist inside, we seek peace and quiet in food.

How many of us have never eaten a candy bar or ice cream or even a meal when we weren't really hungry? Food becomes one of our stress management techniques, and for some, it is their only way of coping.

Stressful Eating

Eating in response to stress and emotions is not wrong or harmful. It is not an act of weakness or illness. It is not necessarily even a problem…unless it is the only choice a person uses to handle stress, pain, and emotional discomfort.

Over-reliance on any one technique, approach, or behavior to help us get through the challenges of our lives simply does not work. No one behavior can suit the needs of every situation. If we have not developed the ability to clearly face our challenges and act appropriately for our feelings and needs, then we are going to muddle through as best we can.

We have to do something, anything to try and at least handle the stress we feel. If we grew up in family systems where our role models had a one-dimensional approach to crisis, then we can do nothing more than mimic that same strategy. Whether we pick food, alcohol, sex, work, etc is almost irrelevant. What is important to recognize is the fact that we never developed the ability to choose other options.

The act of nurturing ourselves with food—which in the most loving sense means taking time to ask ourselves what we need and want and then providing it in a caring and beautiful way—is a conscious and gentle option for self-care that is appropriate for many circumstances.

If all of us approached every act of living—including eating—in this same conscious and gentle manner, our lives would feel full, integrated, and moving forward in a positive, evolutionary way. Few live with such conscious awareness, and those of us who struggle with eating issues have not developed this clarity and focus when we consider our daily choices.

Without real awareness and choice, we cannot have a true sense of identity. We live more like robots, responding to situations in our lives with a pre-programmed pattern of action. We do what is expected of us. We adapt, fit in, and please.

Losing Our Voice

In pleasing, we lose ourselves. We lose the voice that expresses our personal opinions and views. Without practice, ultimately, we lose even the opinions themselves. We dare

> *We do what is expected of us. We adapt, fit in, and please. In pleasing, we lose ourselves. We lose the voice that expresses our personal opinions and views. Without practice, ultimately, we lose even the opinions themselves.*

only say, *I don't know*, when asked to respond to something. We lose the curiosity and sense of adventure that could take us into new dimensions of ourselves. We lose the sense of hope that makes living magical and full of possibility. We lose the very essence that makes us vibrant and alive.

This makes us angry, deeply angry. We have been stripped of our personal lives, and we can't say exactly how it happened. We can't find anyone to blame, and we don't know what is missing. We begin to wonder if we are imagining things, overly sensitive, or worse, crazy.

However we try to accept things as they are, the sense remains that something is deeply wrong. This is not how life should be. We want a life of happiness and success. We want to contribute and make our world a better place. But we feel powerless to begin changing our experience of life and the world.

We eat out of frustration, out of pain, out of hopelessness. We eat to pass the time until a better solution can be found. As long as a spark of hope and defiance remain in our souls, we eat. Those who lose this spark completely, may take their lives in despair.

Crack Of Hope

This spark of hope is a crack in our darkened world. Our eating is a signal that tells everyone clearly that we want things to be different. Our behaviors demand that we find something better. We watch every talk show, read magazines, and listen to people hoping to find a clue: *What is missing? Is this what life is really about? How can I make it different?*

If we stumble upon a healthy situation or relationship such as a good therapeutic relationship, we begin to ask the question "why." Why do I do what I do? This question leads us into a personal search for truth. At some point, we have our first "ah-hah." We see things from a wider viewpoint than ever before.

We learn to see reasons and motivations, cause and effect. We find out that our behavior makes sense considering where we came from. We consider new interpretations for the first time. This begins to free us from the grip of our past and present. We begin to think about ourselves and our lives differently. We find courage to create new options, and we experience power for the first time.

The unfolding of our self-awareness and personal power occurs in layers. It is a slow and magnificent process. Over time, every corner of our beings receive the light and loving attention of this personal growth

process. We are waking from a living slumber. We are finding ourselves.

This process of self-definition is by its very nature spiritual. Asking the questions—*Who am I? Why am I here? What do I want? Where am I going? How can I get there?*—is an act of courage, especially for a woman. All of us have these questions and all of us ask them. Yet few of us pursue them with any real vigor because most of us have been socialized from infancy to please.

Learning To Please

Early on, we learned that our parents responded more positively to our smiles than our cries. We learned that people appreciated us when we were helpful and out of the way. We learned to stand in line and speak when spoken to at school. We learned to fit in.

This socialization filtered away much of the natural excitement, urge to explore, delight in learning, and creative expression which children universally exhibit. Unfortunately, long before adolescence, most of us learned to stick with the crowd.

Young girls, in particular, learn to follow social expectations and thereby lose their individual expressiveness by their early teens. When girls ask themselves questions of self-determination, it naturally leads to new ideas and behaviors. This gets them into trouble. They simply learn not to ask. The voice inside that wonders about things is silenced so that they can fit in perfectly.

Generally, it takes a personal crisis to awaken the willingness to again listen to that inner voice that wonders about things. Only when life's real meaning is on the line do most of us begin a conscious process of sorting out our purpose and values. Starting a new school or job, moving, losing an important relationship, or going through a health crisis can trigger a multitude of questions. By allowing ourselves to question, we step out as individuals, perhaps for the first time.

A Powerful Protest

A person who struggles with eating issues goes through the same process. She feels the same mandates to fit in. She works hard to adapt to the expectations of those around her. She learns early to repress her feelings and opinions to avoid rocking the boat and losing the approval of others. Her individuality is mainstreamed and ultimately submerged. And it takes a crisis for her to change.

Eating problems are often triggered by a major life event that shakes up the person's world. By eating, a person tries to stuff conflictual and painful feelings inside because the issues she faces could upset the established order of her life if dealt with directly. By acting out her stress through her eating behaviors while denying there is anything else at issue, she is working very hard to keep her life stable.

Eating is also a way to safely express anger. Many things upset us, but we do not have a socially-condoned outlet through which to express rage. When we eat with rage, we acknowledge on some level that things are not how they ought to be.

Could emotional eating be the beginning of a personal attempt to evolve beyond society's vision for us? Clearly, we lack the tools and even the vision which can take us beyond our current limits. Our attempts to protest are crude and self-destructive, but powerful nonetheless.

Unless we see eating issues and eating disorders as part of a process to define the self and create a personal identity, we miss the exciting potential it represents. This search to identify the core of the self—to meet it, to get to know it, to accept it, to love it, and to learn how it fits into the larger world—is the essence of personal growth.

Embarking on a personal search for meaning is the beginning of a lifetime process. Where our paths will lead us, what we will find along the way, and what resources we will take with us is impossible to predict.

A search for meaning—by any of us and certainly for a person who suffers with eating difficulties—is not launched overnight. While the journey for everyone is unique, it typically begins in childhood with broken dreams and family pain—in families that just can't talk about real feelings and issues for fear that it might destroy the illusion of accomplishment and togetherness they have tried so hard to create. Everyone feels isolated and without support.

Lonely Families

In these families, people generally have no skills for handling challenge constructively. They have never learned to talk things through. They do not know how to hear all

> *Eating is also a way to safely express anger. Many things upset us, but we do not have a socially-condoned outlet through which to express rage. When we eat with rage, we acknowledge on some level that things are not how they ought to be.*

sides of the story. They take conflict to mean problems, dissent, and breakdown of authority, etc., and they avoid it at all costs.

The cost for maintaining the illusion of harmony where there is none is tremendous. A child in this world learns truth has two sides. Reality cannot be trusted. Everyone acts as if everything is fine, but it's not. She senses the disharmony, but she quickly learns not to say anything or she will be punished in some way. She is firmly told that nothing is wrong. She wants to believe, but no one is happy. A child in this system begins to feel depressed, hopeless, and insecure. She is emotionally alone.

She feels abandoned and unworthy of her parents' affection. She wonders what is so wrong with her to make her family ignore her. She tries everything she can to win their attention and affection, but her efforts are in vain. She begins to hate herself.

These families know that a brandy or homemade pie often takes away the edge of pain for a brief time. During really tough times, more drinking and eating goes on. Children who watched their parents later mimicked these same patterns.

If someone also has learned to respond to personal stress with violence—insults, yelling, physical bruising, or sexual abuse— then the secrets, isolation, and fear are even greater.

Broken Creeds

During this time, she learns about a god that created the world and is supposed to love everything. She learns that love is supreme and that religious people follow commandments to help them act in a more loving, godly way.

She learned these codes, and then quickly learned that many people do not follow them. Neighbors did not act lovingly toward neighbors. Children and elders were not always protected. People did not hold God in the highest priority and act accordingly. Everywhere she looked, the promises for happiness and love she learned to hope for were broken. Whether God was at fault or people were, she was not sure. But what she had been taught did not give her a sense of peace or understanding. In fact, it added to her pain. If God could not be counted on, then what could?

The world beyond her family was also riddled with double messages and flawed goodwill. As she grew older, she had a chance to see many adults in action. She saw parents in the supermarket yell at and hit their kids. She saw her best friend's mother drunk whenever she came over to play. Her teachers said they were there to help, but some insulted students thinking it would

motivate them to study. Some threw kids up against lockers to keep law and order. Some were scared of the tough kids in the class.

At the same time, these people tried to teach her the principles of living and guide her behavior. They set standards for her to achieve. They held the power to grade her which would open or close later doors. Just like in her family, she had to fit in. She had to please them to survive and thrive in their world. She had to deny injustices and act as if everything was fine.

Spiritual Emptiness

She was getting a clear message. Appearance was everything. It really didn't matter what she felt or thought. What mattered was how everything looked. If people looked happy, then they must be. If it looked good and successful, then it must be.

If she wanted to be accepted, she had to play the part. She had to fit in. She learned to figure out what people wanted and give it to them. She learned to adapt, adopt, please— whatever it took. Eventually, she became cynical. If this is really how the world was, what did it matter what she did? No wonder people didn't live according to their principles.

She suffered from a kind of spiritual emptiness. Her life had become a series of costuming events. She put on one show after another for family, friends, teachers, and lovers. She gave them what they wanted to see. She made them happy.

But she herself was not happy. Her world had become very dark, very dead. Nothing inspired her any longer. Her creative enthusiasm left long ago. Every dream she ever had seemed childish now. She had been foolish to hope for love. She was silly to think she would be able to use her talents and find her own place in the world.

Living this way was intolerable, but she knew nothing else. So she kept up her appearances at work, school, and home. No one knew she was dealing with this inner pain. Everything looked fine from the outside—she had learned that lesson well.

Yet she couldn't get rid of her deep disappointment. Some inner place protested and kept looking for a better way.

Empty Eating

Long ago, she had learned to eat for comfort. Her mother had fed her when she bruised her knees and came home crying. Feeding was her family's way of loving. She learned that to feel comfort, she had to eat. For years, she reached for food to fill her up and calm down her inner turmoil.

As she grew older, eating remained one of the only dependable elements of her life. As her pain grew, so did her eating. As she branched out into new experiences, it was difficult to keep up with everyone's conflicting expectations. She wasn't sure any longer who she should be. It had been so much simpler when she had to only please her family, teacher, and a few friends. Now, she was stretched much farther and often felt like she would come apart at the seams.

To get away from it all, she would indulge herself even more. She felt shameful for having
this secret release, but she needed it so desperately. It was the only time she felt nourished.

At some point, her eating outstripped her budget, her body, and her lifestyle. She could no longer afford the quantities of food she required to escape. Her body was feeling the effects of her repeated behaviors, and she was afraid. She withdrew from her friends and she started missing work and school. Her eating now threatened to destroy the appearance of success she was trying so hard to maintain.

Ready To Change

She began to get really frightened—and angry. This had to stop. This is not how things should be. She had tried all of her life to be good, and now look what had become of her. Was life supposed to be this meaningless and empty? Was life nothing other than one endless box of chocolates?

Her anger began to mobilize her. She began to look for clues from anything in her environment. She didn't know what kind of clues they might be—she just hoped she would recognize them at the time.

Something triggered her decision to try therapy. Perhaps it was an afternoon talk show or an article in the paper. She had seen some ads for therapists talking about eating, so she tried them first. She made her first appointment. It was the beginning of a long process.

Awakening does not always begin with or even necessarily require any formal therapeutic experience. To wake up, one needs to find out: *What is inside? Who am*

> *Unless she learned a new way of living, she would keep repeating the patterns. She vowed not to get stuck. Since she had learned these things, she could unlearn them.*

I? What do I feel? What do I need? How do I get those needs met? What do I want? How can I get these things? Finding the answers to these questions has the potential to heal life pain.

One day, she has a shocking realization. She is living out a pattern of behaviors she learned from her family. She never learned constructive ways to cope. She saw the adults in her early years deny problems and pain and then reach for something to numb what they were feeling. She realized that she was set up to do the same thing when food and comfort were synonymous in early childhood. She could only repeat what she learned and saw around her.

Releasing The Past

She felt less shame about this once it dawned on her that there were reasons for what she did. Unless she learned a new way of living, she would keep repeating the patterns. She vowed not to get stuck. Since she had learned these things, she could unlearn them.

She also began acknowledging how past events made her feel. The pain she had tried so hard to numb all those years was finally surfacing. She now knew why it was there. Her therapeutic and support resources helped give her courage to face old feelings, accept what happened, comfort herself in new ways, and move on.

Letting in old feelings in order to let go of them took great courage and energy. Sometimes it was all too much and she found herself eating. She learned to see the connection between food and feelings and understand that her eating had comforted, protected, and even informed her. It now became a signal that deeper issues needed to be handled.

She felt like she was backsliding at these times. Certainly, she wanted to be beyond the power of food, but she wasn't. But this time, her backslide did not make her give up. She kept exploring. She was ferociously afraid at the beginning. What if this was all in vain? She could not tolerate another disappointment. But something inside made her feel like she was going in the right direction. She felt real optimism for the first time in a long time. She knew she was stumbling about like a toddler taking her first steps, but nevertheless, she was moving.

Models, Maps & Mentors

But where was she going? Clearly, she needed a map. She needed a vision to help her recognize the right turns along the way. She read new books. She listened to people talk. She discussed her emerging ideas and dreams with her therapist. She wanted models and mentors that could help her define what she wanted in life.

She experimented with everything. Things which stayed the longest and the easiest felt right. At first she rushed around to find the answers right away. She needed the security so badly, that she wanted to change overnight. Instead, she learned from her spurts of progress and periods of regression that this was going to take time.

As she tried out new things, she learned about her power of choice. She founds things she liked and didn't. Some things worked and others failed miserably. This was true for food and eating behaviors as well as every other dimension of her life. She was beginning to learn about her tastes and needs. She had opinions and preferences. She was exhilarated! She had her self back!

As she grew, the grip of her obsessive eating was lessening. That didn't mean she didn't feel impulses to eat—she did. She was just learning that she had the ability to choose whether she was going to eat or not.

Each successful choice helped her to trust herself. She began to feel certain that she could count on herself. She did not feel as alone anymore. She was beginning to feel like a whole person. All of this stumbling about had had a purpose.

Eventually, her life began to feel more normal. As she got better, so did her relationships, school, and work. She felt budding pride in how far she had come and happiness at her new life

The Journey Continues

For some people, the quest stops here. They have created a healthier lifestyle by working hard and finding resources—both inner and outer—they can turn to when they need shoring up. They do not take their return to wellness for granted. They know that they have to remain committed to dealing with personal challenge in a conscious and on-going manner. They move into a maintenance phase and proceed with their lives.

For others, re-establishing a normal lifestyle is not enough. Their healing process has opened the doorway to their inner selves and they discover a great joy in finding out who they are. Each step they take helps them discover more about themselves. They uncover layers they never knew existed. They find strength they never knew they had. They learn patience and love little by little. This journey is the richest, most interesting experience they ever had. Giving it up just because they have the ability to choose when and what to eat and how to cope with personal challenge made no sense. They have not yet learned everything about themselves nor have they exhausted their potential for developing perspectives, talents, and creative expression. They continue with their personal search. Growing becomes the purpose of their lives.

At some point early or later on in the healing process, most individuals have to come face to face with a pain that is larger than the hurt they experienced from any family member, acquaintance, or stranger regardless of the degree of abuse. They have to deal with feelings of betrayal and abandonment from God.

However each of us envisions the creative force of the universe, when we see people go through tremendous pain, eventually we ask "why?." Often this questioning is directed toward outward injustices such as problems of homelessness, the environment, racial inequity, political corruption, starvation, etc. It is harder to ask the question about our own lives.

Pain Of Injustice

But when a person finally opens herself up to the pain of neglect, abuse, and emotional trauma, the sorrow and rage is deep and raw. Over time, she can make peace by understanding the abuse and neglect her elders experienced and then passed on out of ignorance and pain.

For some, this understanding is enough. For others, they eventually wonder why the

world was ever set up this way in the first place. How each person answers this difficult question is absolutely unique. They may draw on religious upbringing for a model. They may begin learning about other philosophies and systems of thought because what they were taught in church and school doesn't provide enough answers.

Luckily, in our time, there is a great deal of spiritual exploration so each person should be able to find something that resonates with her.

As she seeks models and mentors to help her sort out the meaning of things, she finds elements that fit her emerging values and belief system. She weaves these elements into a framework of explanations that works for her. The explanations help her know the purpose of her life, the reasons why she has been through the experiences she has had,

> *As she seeks models and mentors to help her sort out the meaning of things, she finds elements that fit her emerging values and belief system. She weaves these elements into a framework of explanations that works for her.*

the directions in which she'll head, and what qualities to look for in the people and lifestyle she chooses for support.

In seeking answers to the most fundamental questions of where we come from, why we are here, and where we are going, each of us has to decide how the universe came to be and what the fundamental nature of life is all about. We have to tackle and tussle with issues such as good versus evil, pleasure versus pain, perfection versus sin, and other spiritual issues: *Is there a god? Is god good? Are people good? Why do we hurt each other? What can we do about it? How can we find peace?*

Humans have been asking these questions for as long as we know. They appear to be important to give meaning to life. It is through this discovery process that the inner spirit or core being of the person becomes recognized and integrated.

The Truth Within

The inner being is deeper than the emotional self. It is on a more silent level beyond words and feelings. This inner being nourishes the mind and heart. Its submerged quality makes it seem invisible, but many speak of a kind of knowing that can't be explained. We have to trust this knowing. It comes from a purer, more innocent and often very wise part of ourselves. When the truth is heard and followed, a person often feels more whole, more connected to all parts of herself. She feels more harmonious, and her actions are more in keeping with her values.

It often takes quiet, private activities to begin to access this part of the self. Journal writing. Walking in the woods. Meditation. Prayer. Playing wordless music. Solitary running. Lap swimming. Sitting in moonlight. Watching sunsets.

By building in private time for reading, writing, and thinking about larger issues and listening to the inner self, a person comes to understand these universal and spiritual questions. Now, she has to trust her own growth. She has the tools. She has the will. She knows how to find help when she needs it. The rest of her journey will be into ever new territory. Some of it will be easy and some very difficult as it always has been. But she will reap great rewards for her effort to know the truth of her life and soul.

We are in a time of great social change. Even the earth herself seems to be changing. Much of what worked in the past is under question now, and none of us are sure about what lies ahead.

In such a time, the only response we can possibly have—besides burying our heads in one way or another—is to at least take care of our own growth. The arena where we can effect the most change is right here within ourselves. As we get clearer and stronger, the impact of our actions on those we love and those we come into contact with during our days will be greater and more positive. If every human being made it his or her first priority to heal body, mind, heart, and soul, we would have a very different world out there.

Resources

It is time that women start making peace with their bodies and learn loving and constructive ways for nurturing themselves—other than by eating or starving. Having uplifting and positive information that models healthier alternatives for healing and growing is important for all women.

*The **EASE™ Living to Grow™ Resources** are dedicated to helping women of all ages begin to change their relationships to food and their bodies as well as create healthier, more fulfilling lives for themselves. Let us know if you wish to learn more about these tools to help you enrich your personal journey.*

It's easy to do. Call 1-800-470-GROW or visit us at www.livingtogrow.com.

The EASE™ Living to Grow™ Resources

www.livingtogrow.com

Dance Naked in Your Living Room: Handling Stress & Finding Joy

by Rebecca Ruggles Radcliffe

by Rebecca Ruggles Radcliffe
www.livingtogrow.com
(800) 470-GROW (4769)
At bookstores and online
or send $12 + $3 s/h to
EASE, PO Box 8032
Mpls, MN 55408
ISBN# 0-9636607-1-3

Dance Naked In Your Living Room is a playful, joyful, and inspirational book for women who are feeling stress in their personal lives. We use food to cope because we haven't learned other constructive ways to nurture or care for ourselves. There isn't enough "stress education" in our schools or on the job. So we turn repeatedly to the old habits that soothe us—until we learn something new. *Dance Naked* helps us find moments of joy for ourselves--in spite of the pressured lives we lead today.

...Living Room show us how stress drains our energy and hope...and ...20 wonderful ways to nurture ourselves. This way, in a few short ...own and find peace instead of overeating—and/or overshopping, getting ...and alone, orturning to alcohol or drugs! The *Dance Naked* ...ck, easy, free, and feel good. By using *Dance Naked*, we can ...ments of joy, connection, and grace in our lives.

...you love the gift of the health, wellness, and joy of *Dance Naked In* ...nd remember, it is a perfect little book for birthdays, anniversaries, office occasions, Mother's Day, Father's Day, Bosses and Secretary/Associates' Day, and Valentine's Day celebrations!

"Together, Dance Naked In Your Living Room, and Enlightened Eating, and Body Prayers: Finding Body Peace offer a comprehensive and insightful approach to changing stress and emotional eating!"

"Anyone who feels stress deserves Dance Naked!"

159

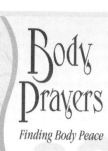

Body Prayers: Finding Body Peace– A Journey of Self Acceptance

Body Prayers takes us on an insightful journey which questions our impossible standards of thinness that lead to intolerance, low self-esteem, body hatred, and disordered eating. This highly sensitive and personal inside look at how women view themselves and their bodies is combined with powerful statistics to help us shift away from impossibly thin expectations toward acceptance of body diversity. Poems, 'prayers,' and affirmations gently close the book.

"Thank you for writing this book!" "It has been helpful in my group!"

Enlightened Eating™: Understanding and Changing Your Relationship With Food

A special book on eating, overeating, weight, and body-image that explores the link between stress, eating, emotions, and self-esteem. It gently inspires and encourages readers to discover their inner needs and emotions and make healthier life choices. ***Enlightened Eating*** includes 34 exercises for an individual or group to promote insight & change. It has sections on women's growth, spirituality, surviving holidays, stress, and emotional eating filled with beautiful quotes and affirmations.

"This is the best book I've read on the subject!" "I use it with our disordered eating group at the rape crisis center. It really helps."

Body Wisdom Set

The wisdom of ***Enlightened Eating***, ***Dance Naked***, and ***Body Prayers*** is combined into one extraordinary and revolutionary set for women with insight on emotional eating, stress management, and body acceptance. A $6 savings on the set!

About to Burst: Handling Stress & Ending Violence Kids today have more pressure than ever; but many do not have constructive ways to let off steam other than alcohol, drugs, aggression, eating disorders, depression, etc. Written in response to the disturbing school shootings —a symptom of rising stress, violence and rage in our society, *About to Burst* teaches young people ways of unwinding before they blow. Learning stress skills is a critical violence prevention solution, and it gives young people healthy options they can use the rest of their lives.

"Timely insight for a most difficult problem."

Developing Healthier Eating Habits* helps anyone begin to make positive change. A practical pocket-guide to creating new eating patterns. 12,000+ used by counselors, colleges, and health professionals. Excellent handout./Bulk rates. (*Special offer: 1 free copy with any book/tape order!)

"A fabulous help for those with eating or body concerns!"

Enlightened Eating Tape Set has four heart-warming, uplifting, and introductory discussions to trigger new insights and understanding. Topics include emotional eating, body hatred, eating disorders, and the search for meaning.

"Such a private and easy tool to introduce sensitive concepts!"

Keeping Current Talks are live recordings of Rebecca's lively, popular talks. $10 per tape.
Dance Naked In Your Living Room, Freeport Health System, IL 2/99 (1 tape)
Finding Body Peace, North Memorial Women's Center, MN, 11/99 (2 tapes)
Living to Grow: Working Women's Summit, ND, 10/99 (1 tape)
Dare to Dream: Working women's Summit, ND 10/99 (1 tape)
Learning to Live in Our Bodies, Women's History Month, Middlebury College, VT, 11/98 (1 tape)
Supporting Women's Journeys in the New Millennium, Women's History Month, Florida Community College, 3/2000 (1 tape)
Eating Disorders Awareness Week 1998, Murray College, KY 2/98 (1 tape)
Celebrating Every Body Week 1999, University of Nebraska-Lincoln, 2/99 (1 tape)
Eating Disorders Awareness Week 2000, Quinsigamond Community College, MA, 4/2000 (1 tape)
Wellness & Eating Disorders Week 2000, Mercyhurst College, 3/2000 (1 tape)
Making an Impact: Helping Women Come to Healthy Terms with Food, Weight, & Bodies, Central WA Univ, 2/2000 (2 tapes)
Calming the Chaos: Women Coping with Stress in a Changing Future, Grand View Hospital, Sellarsville, PA, 3/2000 (1 tape)
Silent Scream: The Inner Violence of Eating Disorders, Onondaga Valley Mental Health Association, NY, 4/2000 (1 tape)

Anorexia & Bulimia: The Silent Struggle is a compassionate and intimate video discussion of what eating disorders are, how they affect the body, what causes these problems, what kind of help someone needs, and what a loved one can do to support recovery. 29 mns. Suitable for small group or individual viewing only. Previews/rentals not available at this price.

"A compassionate introduction to eating disorders and the struggle to recover."

Living to Grow: Workshops & Talks
Presented by Rebecca Ruggles Radcliffe

Rebecca Ruggles Radcliffe's inspiration and wisdom can be shared with audiences around the country. She believes women today can become anything they choose. Yet she knows the pressure we all feel to live up to social expectations is enormous—leaving us vulnerable to stress and plagued with low self-esteem. Sadly, many of us focus on managing appearance to compensate for a sense of inadequacy and being overwhelmed. Rebecca's heart-warming and honest presentations uplift audiences and provide encouragement to grow. Her talks touch the hearts of large or small groups, professionals, women of all ages, employees, and the general community. Some of her most popular talks are described below.

It is time for a new vision for all— one in which we celebrate and accept ourselves and the gifts we have for the world. Rebecca Ruggles Radcliffe

Learning To Live In Our Bodies: Untangling Emotions, Food, and Body-Hatred
Rebecca asserts that women do not have to be thin and perfectly fit to be vibrant, happy, and fulfilled. She explores why so many of us have learned to hate our bodies and spend endless time, energy, and money trying to control weight—instead of using our talents to enrich our lives and better the world. A powerful antidote to the body shame and depression that deeply affects so many!

Dance Naked In Your Living Room
Rebecca gives a light-hearted, uplifting talk or workshop on finding moments of joy and being good to ourselves. This is a delightful way to enhance our coping and self-nurturing skills—as well as an essential part of dealing with the inner stress that often leads to eating and body image concerns.

Living To Grow: Choosing To Be Conscious, Courageous, and Creative
Rebecca reflects deeply on key issues facing women in their search for happiness, authenticity, and personal power. Examining the exponential cultural changes of the 20th century which deeply affected women's lives and looking toward the rapidly changing future, this presentation inspires women to seek personal growth as the doorway to unfolding life purpose and fulfillment.

Finding Body Peace: A Journey of Self Acceptance
Rebecca inspires women to consider a path of tolerance and self-appreciation toward the wonderful bodies that carry us through our lives. In a gentle combination of affirmation, alternate imaging, and warm-hearted ritual, she helps us to find a spirit of self-acceptance and body appreciation.

Skinny Dreams: Stress, Eating, & Success
Rebecca examines how extreme standards of thinness erode self-esteem and undermine women's success. She advocates for size tolerance and diversity so that we can be free to pursue dreams instead of being tied to the scale.

Hot Flashes, Chocolate Sauce, & Rippled Thigh: Body Image for Real Women
A fabulous, fun affirmation of adult womens' journeys with their bodies, self-esteem, growth, & the possibilities of age. This is a lively exploration of body image for women past the Barbie doll years, the need for positive self-care, and the deep satisfaction that comes with creating an authentic self.

Making an Impact: Helping Women Find Peace with their Bodies, Eating & Weight

Many clients, patients, & students struggle with cultural dictates that have led to wide-spread dieting, body-hatred, weight and eating problems, and low self-esteem. We must provide women with a new vision for viewing themselves, life experiences, and their bodies to counteract the destructive messages they see and hear. As we teach women healthier ways to nurture themselves and help give voice to their dreams, the impact is deep and powerful.

Body Wisdom: A Journey of Insight & Peace

Rebecca's gentle workshop helps women explore and change attitudes toward their bodies, eating, and dreams. By tuning into their needs, listening to deeper dreams, discovering acceptance, and choosing healthy ways to support their journeys, women move along a holistic path of change, growth, and joy.

Additional Presentations
- Enlightened Eating: Understanding & Changing Your Relationship With Food
- Beyond the Binge: Stress, Tests, and Vending Machines— Surviving College Life (and 'The Freshman 20')
- Lost in a Box of Chocolates: Using Food to Cope
- Visual Bytes: How Media Images Hurt Female Self Esteem

- Bellies, Boobs, & Buttocks: A Closer Look at Body Hatred
- Surviving the Holidays: The Power of New Beginnings
- Stress and Women: Overloaded in the Superwoman Culture
- Anorexia and Bulimia: The Silent Struggle
- A Silent Scream: The Inner Violence of Eating Disorders
- Living to 150! Finding Purpose, Meaning, & vitality
- A Gift to be Simple: Down-Sizing Life Stress
- Women's Wellness: A Matter of Balance
- Daring to Dream: Awakening the Voice of the Soul
- New Millennium, New Rules: work, Wonder, & Wisdom
- Creating Peace: One Person, One Moment at a Time

For Your Special Event

Presentations/Talks	In-Services
Keynotes	PTAs
Conferences	Commencements
Panel Discussions	Classes
Workshops	Orientation
Wellness Fairs	Residence Life Training
Women's Events	Eating Awareness Week
Luncheon Lectures	Assemblies
Women's Health Month	Addiction & Recovery

For More Information
Rebecca has spoken to thousands of women of all ages at varied sites. To discuss designing a program for your organization, call Rebecca Ruggles Radcliffe at 1-800-470-4769 or www.livingtogrow.com.

Audience Comments:

"You are riveting!"

"...exactly what I needed..."

"Everything you said hit home, point after point"

"You tell a truth that we all recognize but few dare talk about."

"This reinforced the changes I am making in my life."

"Very empowering!"

"You have a remarkable ability to engage an audience."

"Your compassion and sensitivity really shows."

"You speak to us on our level–and talk about things we really feel."

Discovering The Truth: How We Feel About Bodies, Food & Weight

Dear Friend:

Women of all ages share concerns about their bodies and weight which are never voiced. Sadly, this often leaves us feeling alone—and seemingly overly concerned about body size. Yet our society remains obsessed with thinness—and oblivious to the detrimental effect it has on esteem. I need your help to detail these concerns and foster honest discussion about how damaging it is for women. Would you please anonymously answer the following key questions about body image, weight, and the use of food for comfort? Thank you!! Please copy this and pass it on to other women (ages 14-74+!) and men (for comparison and discover about male issues) you know. I appreciate your help.

Please return questionnaires to EASE™, P.O. Box 8032, Minneapolis, MN 55408. The answers will be pooled anonymously and used to build awareness and educate the public about body image, food, and weight. All information is private and confidential. EASE does not sell its mailing list. If you wish to receive the results of the survey, please include your name and permanent address at the end—or send a separate request. We will also add you to the EASE mailing list. ***Thank you.***

1. Do you have more than one size clothing (fat or skinny clothes) in your closet?
   ❒ yes   ❒ no

2. Have you ever bought an article of clothing that was too small to motivate yourself to lose weight?
   ❒ yes   ❒ no

3. Do you frequently begin diets on Monday mornings?
   ❒ yes   ❒ no

4. Do you ever skip breakfast or lunch to reduce the number of calories you eat in a day?
   ❒ yes   ❒ no

5. Do you honestly wish that you were:
   ❒ 5-10 pounds lighter?
   ❒ 15-20 pounds lighter?
   ❒ 35-30 pounds lighter?
   ❒ 45-40 pounds lighter?
   ❒ more than 40 pounds lighter?

6. Do you like the shape and size of your:
   breasts?   ❒ yes   ❒ no
   waist?   ❒ yes   ❒ no
   hips?   ❒ yes   ❒ no
   buttocks?   ❒ yes   ❒ no
   thighs?   ❒ yes   ❒ no

7. Are you comfortable in a bathing suit?
   ❒ yes   ❒ no

8. Do you do most of your emotional eating:
   ❒ in front of the TV?
   ❒ in your car?
   ❒ in your bedroom?
   ❒ alone in the kitchen?

9. To get rid of calories, have you ever:
   ❒ vomited?
   ❒ taken laxatives?
   ❒ skipped meals?
   ❒ exercised?

10. Do you vomit regularly (more than once a week)?
    ❒ yes   ❒ no
    If yes, how many times? _____

11. Do you take laxatives regularly (more than once a week)?
    ❒ yes   ❒ no
    If yes, how many times? _____

12. Do you skip meals regularly (more than once a week)?
    ❒ yes   ❒ no
    If yes, how many times? _____

13. Do you exercise regularly (more than once a week)?
    ❒ yes   ❒ no
    If yes, how many times per week?
    _____
    And for how long each session on average? _____

14. How old were you when you dieted for the first time?
    _____

15. Did your mother diet regularly?
    ❒ yes   ❒ no

16. Was she self-conscious about her weight?
    ❒ yes   ❒ no

17. Was she concerned about your weight?
    ❒ yes   ❒ no

18. Did she ever tease or belittle you about your weight?
    ❒ yes   ❒ no

19. Did your father diet regularly?
    ❒ yes   ❒ no

20. Was he self-conscious about his weight?
    ❒ yes   ❒ no

21. Was he concerned about your weight?
    ❒ yes   ❒ no

22. Did he ever tease or belittle you about your weight?
    ❒ yes   ❒ no

23. Do you binge (over-indulge)
    ❒ food?
    ❒ on shopping?
    ❒ on drinking alcohol?
    ❒ on using non-prescribed drugs?
    ❒ on work?
    ❒ on sex?
    ❒ on exercise?

24. Did you have a weight problem as a child?
    ❑ yes   ❑ no

25. Did anyone else in your family have a weight problem? (check all that apply)
    ❑ Mother
    ❑ Father
    ❑ Sister(s)
    ❑ Brother(s)
    ❑ Grandmother(s)
    ❑ Grandfather(s)
    ❑ Aunt(s)
    ❑ Uncle(s)

26. Does your weight fluctuate up and down more than 5 pounds within a month's time?
    ❑ yes   ❑ no

27. Do you find it harder to lose weight each time you diet?
    ❑ yes   ❑ no

28. Do you end up a few pounds heavier after a diet?
    ❑ yes   ❑ no

29. Have you ever tried:
    ❑ prescription liquid diets?
    ❑ over-the-counter liquid diets?
    ❑ Weight Watchers
    ❑ Overeaters Anonymous?
    ❑ Jenny Craig?
    ❑ Nutri system?
    ❑ Ultra Slim Fast?

30. When you lose weight, are you able to keep it off indefinitely?
    ❑ yes   ❑ no

31. If no, what do you believe is the reason?
    ❑ Lack of willpower
    ❑ Lack of support
    ❑ Diet didn't address real problems
    ❑ Other people's poor eating habits
    ❑ Other _____
    ❑ Other _____
    ❑ Other _____
    ❑ Other _____

32. Over the years, what have you used to help you manage your weight?
    ❑ Medical Doctors
    ❑ Magazine Diets
    ❑ Liquid Diets
    ❑ Overeaters Anonymous
    ❑ Weight Watchers
    ❑ Weight Camp
    ❑ New Year's Resolutions

❑ Exercise
❑ Keeping Busy
❑ Rewards & Bribes
❑ Dieting With A Buddy
❑ Fasting
❑ Skipping Meals
❑ Controlling Portion Size
❑ Taboo Foods (avoiding chips, chocolate, potatoes, etc.)
❑ Empty Cupboards/Refrigerator
❑ Diet Foods
❑ Eating Disorder Programs
❑ Counseling
❑ Religion
❑ Prayer
❑ Hypnosis
❑ Political/Environmental Cause
❑ Love
❑ Nutritionist

33. Do you eat more than your body needs for activity?
    ❑ yes   ❑ no

34. Do you eat more frequently than your body needs to eat?
    ❑ yes   ❑ no

35. When you are eating for reasons other than physical hunger, why do you think you eat? (check all that apply and rank order with 1 being the reason you eat most frequently)
    ❑ Stressed   ❑ Lonely
    ❑ Unhappy   ❑ Frustrated
    ❑ Bored   ❑ Overwhelmed
    ❑ Angry   ❑ Frightened
    ❑ Isolated   ❑ Disappointed
    ❑ Ashamed   ❑ Peaceful
    ❑ Happy   ❑ Satisfied
    ❑ Calm   ❑ Accomplished
    ❑ Excited   ❑ Sensual
    ❑ Loved   ❑ Aroused

36. How old were you when you began eating for emotional reasons? _____
    _____
    _____

37. Do you eat to:
    ❑ reward yourself?
    ❑ comfort yourself?
    ❑ soothe yourself?
    ❑ punish yourself?
    ❑ calm yourself?
    ❑ energize yourself?
    ❑ distract yourself?
    ❑ entertain yourself?
    ❑ block out thoughts and feelings?
    ❑ blank out the world?
    ❑ unwind?

38. What do you feel could really make a difference about how you use food to cope? _____
    _____
    _____

    about managing weight? _____
    _____
    _____

    about making peace with your body size and shape? _____
    _____
    _____
    _____

39. For survey analysis, please tell us your:

    Age_____ Hgt_____ Wgt _____

    Sex: M_____ F _____

    Clothing Size   _____

    Highest Weight   _____

    Goal Weight   _____

    Lowest Weight   _____

    Race   _____

Please return the survey to: EASE™, PO Box 8032, Minneapolis, MN 55408.

Thanks!

Becky

If you would like the results of the survey and to be on the EASE mailing list, please fill in the following information— or send a separate request:

Name _____

Address _____

_____

City _____

State_____

Zip _____

Thank you!

About Rebecca Ruggles Radcliffe

*R*ebecca Ruggles Radcliffe is a national speaker and consultant on women's issues, stress management, personal growth, self-esteem, body image, emotional eating, eating disorders, spirituality, simplicity, professional/personal balance, and violence prevention. Since 1988, she has been Executive Director of EASE™ Publications & Resources, whose mission is to enhance personal growth. She is author of ***Dance Naked In Your Living Room: Handling Stress & Finding Joy***, ***Enlightened Eating: Understanding & Changing Your Relationship With Food***, ***Body Prayers: Finding Body Peace—A Journey of Self Acceptance***, the ***Body Wisdom Set***, and ***About to Burst: Handling Stress & Ending Violence*** along with many tapes and other support tools. In addition, she is working on new books which will be announce on the website and through annual mailings. To be added to the mailing list, use the form in the book or at www.livingtogrow.com.

Ms. Radcliffe is an Adjunct Faculty Member of St. Mary's University, has her graduate degree from the University of St. Thomas and undergraduate degrees from the University of Minnesota, and is former VP of The Renfrew Center, a treatment facility for eating disorders and women's well-being. Rebecca avidly practices life-balancing strategies, seeks avenues for growth in her home and work life, plans to live to 200 years, and is mother to a strong, creative, and opinionated daughter.

Rebecca is a powerful, engaging author and speaker who helps shed light and reframe current issues affecting us all. Thinking deeply about this special time in our history, she has a gift for sharing a perspective that uplifts and compassionately inspires us to reach for our highest dreams and potential. Whether speaking to college or school audiences, addressing professional, community or corporate groups, Rebecca's humor, warmth, and personal approach shines as she explores ideas important to today.

Please check ***www.livingtogrow.com*** for updated information on Rebecca's activities and publications.

Acknowledgements

Over the years, many people have helped me learn to write, to be willing to use my voice, and dare to pursue my dreams; thank you to all of them. In particular, I cannot close this book without a special thank you to my sister, Beth, whose faithful dedication and creative talent gave me the beautiful design for *Enlightened Eating,* and to my father who read the book twice, cover to cover, and said this book is really about being human. I also thank the many individuals and professionals who have shared how much this work means to them. I appreciate hearing from each and every one of you.